HOW TO KNOW GOD

Crusade Messages 2004—2005

GREG LAURIE

ALLEN DAVID BOOKS

KERYGMA™ PUBLISHING Dana Point, California

HOW TO
KNOW GOD
GREG LAURIE

ISBN 0-977103-1-9
Printed in United States of America

Published by: Kerygma Publishing–Dana Point, California
Coordination: FM Management, Ltd.
Cover design: Christopher Laurie
Editor: Karla Pedrow
Interior Design, Production: Highgate Cross+Cathey, Ltd.

Table of **Contents**

God's Cure **for Heart Trouble**

Have you ever felt stressed-out to the max, where it seemed like everything went wrong—all at once? Then, when it seemed like it could not get worse, it did? Or, let me put it another way: Do you have kids? And more to the point, do you have teenagers? Then you know what I'm talking about.

One of the downsides of the information age in which we have our cell phones, PDAs, BlackBerries, Treos, and even watches that can send and receive the latest data is that we are barraged by information. That gives us even more to worry and be stressed about. And stress is serious stuff. Studies have suggested that high levels of stress can lead to obesity and trigger a raft of diseases, from heart attacks to ulcers. Depression, nervous breakdowns, and even cancer can be stress-related. In the U.S., up to 90 percent of visits to physicians may be triggered by a stress-related illness, according to the Centers for Disease Control and Prevention.[1]

> As Christians, regardless of what cause we may have to be troubled, there is greater cause not to be.

We are stressed out by the many frightening things in our world today. Since 9/11, there are certain fears all Americans have. A March 2005 Associated Press article stated, "Though the Soviet Union is gone, the nuclear fears that fueled the Cold War haven't disappeared.

Most Americans think nuclear weapons are so dangerous that no country should have them, and a majority believe it's likely that terrorists or a nation will use them within five years."[2]

North Korea claims to possess nuclear weapons and to be manufacturing more. Iran is widely believed to be within months of developing such weapons. And lurking in the background is the threat that worries U.S. officials the most: the desire on the part of terrorists to acquire nuclear weapons. All that helps to explain why 52 percent of Americans think a nuclear attack by one country against another is somewhat likely or very likely by 2010, according to an Associated Press poll. And 53 percent of Americans think a nuclear attack by terrorists is at least somewhat likely. That brings us stress, worry, and fear.

God has given us a user's manual for life called the Bible.

You may know of someone who has a fear of heights, small spaces, or flying. But according to a *Time* magazine cover article on the topic of fear, people have phobias for just about everything imaginable. According to the article, over 50 million people in the U.S. have some kind of fear or phobia. Some are pretty unusual, if not slightly humorous. For example, there is kathisophobia, the fear of sitting; ablutophobia, the fear of bathing; dentophobia, the fear of dentists; allodoxaphobia, the fear of opinions; and cyclophobia, the fear of bicycles. And they get even weirder. There is alektorophobia, the fear of chickens; anuptaphobia, the fear of staying single; arachibutyrophobia, the fear of peanut butter sticking to the roof of your mouth; automatonophobia, the fear of ventriloquist dummies; lutraphobia, the fear of otters; ecclesiophobia, the fear of church; hadephobia, the fear of hell; ouranophobia, the fear of heaven; and peladophobia, the fear of baldness and bald people. Finally, there is my personal favorite: phobophobia, which is the fear of phobias.[3]

Perhaps your life is filled with fear, worry, and intense stress right now. Without a doubt, life is certainly filled with troubles. Job 5:7 tells us, "Man is born to trouble."

Disappointment is a trouble, and there are many disappointments. We are disappointed with ourselves, because we are not always what we want to be. We want to be strong, but we are weak. We want to be successful, yet we experience many failures. We want to be loved, but people often are indifferent toward us.

Circumstances also can be a source of trouble, whether it's the loss of a job, things simply not going the way we want them to, and even uncertainty about the future. There are a lot of things that can cause us to be stressed out and afraid.

But my intention is not to add to your stress. Instead, I want to share with you the words of Jesus to stressed-out, agitated people. It is God's cure for heart trouble:

> "Let not your heart be troubled; you believe in God, believe also in Me. In My Father's house are many mansions; if it were not so, I would have told you. I go to prepare a place for you. And if I go and prepare a place for you, I will come again and receive you to Myself; that where I am, there you may be also. And where I go you know, and the way you know." Thomas said to Him, "Lord, we do not know where You are going, and how can we know the way?" Jesus said to him, "I am the way, the truth, and the life. No one comes to the Father except through Me. (John 14:1–6)

At this point, the disciples were afraid. Jesus had just revealed that Judas Iscariot would betray Him. Not only that, but He had told them Simon Peter would deny Him. Then the bombshell: He was going to leave them! They did not understand that He would die on the cross for them and that He would soon live in their hearts. They only heard the part about His leaving. And that caused stress, worry, and fear. The phrase, "Let not your heart be troubled," in verse 1 could be translated, "Don't be agitated, disturbed, or thrown into confusion." Or, "Don't let your heart shudder!" "Troubled" is a picturesque word and also a strong one. Jesus was specifically saying to the disciples, in light of the imminent cross, "It may look like your world is falling apart and that darkness will overtake you, but don't let your heart be troubled!" Notice He didn't say, "Mull over your problems." Instead, He said, "Don't be troubled." And then He laid out three reasons why. As Christians, regardless of what cause we may have to be troubled, there is greater cause *not to be.*

> No matter what happens to you on this earth,
> it pales in comparison to this great hope.

Which brings us to God's first cure for heart trouble: Take Him at His Word. Jesus said, "Believe also in Me" (v. 1). In the original Greek, this is a command. Jesus was saying, "Believe that I know what I'm doing here! My Word is true. You will see that in time."

God has given us a user's manual for life called the Bible. Now, I don't know about you, but I hate to read user's manuals. This is a problem, because I also love electronic gadgets. I always end up doing the one thing you should not do.

But if you are like me, you try out your gadgets first and then read the directions later (and usually end up doing the first thing the user's manual told you not to do!).

While many products come with user's manuals, there are also many products that come with warning labels. Some are helpful, but others seem just plain ridiculous. Of course, those labels probably are there because someone, somewhere did what the label warns you not to do. Consider these true, but goofy, warning labels. A cardboard sun shade for windshields had this warning: "Do not drive with sun shield in place." This warning came with a hair dryer: "Do not use while sleeping." An electric rotary tool warned, "This product not intended for use as a dental drill" A warning on a bathroom heater states, "This product is not to be used in bathrooms." A manual for a microwave oven contains this warning: "Do not use for drying pets." This statement was found on a box of rat poison: "Warning: has been found to cause cancer in laboratory mice." A label on children's cough medicine cautions, "Do not drive or operate machinery." A string of Christmas lights says, "For indoor or outdoor use only." A child-sized Superman costume comes with this warning: "Wearing of this garment does not enable you to fly." A sign at a railroad station declares, "Beware! To touch these wires is instant death. Anyone found doing so will be prosecuted." A shipment of hammers came with the notice, "May be harmful if swallowed." And a bottle of sleeping pills forewarns, "May cause drowsiness."

Think of the crazy people who tried to dry their hair while they were asleep, dry their pets in the microwave, or tried to fly because they were wearing an "S" on their chest. If only they had read the directions and warning labels first!

The same is true of life. The Bible gives us direction and warnings to guide us. In 2 Timothy 3:16–17 we read, "All Scripture is inspired by God and is useful to teach us what is true and to make us realize what is wrong in our lives. It straightens us out and teaches us to do what is right. It is God's way of preparing us in every way, fully equipped for every good thing God wants us to do" (NLT).

Jesus has gone to prepare a place for us.
That is a key element of our comfort.

It reminds me of a true story I heard about a young man who was graduating from college. It was his hope that his father would give him a new car for his graduation present. Many of the other graduates were getting new cars from their dads, so this young man wanted one too. He had even picked out the car he wanted and told his father about it. When the day of his graduation finally arrived, this young man was shocked when his dad did not hand him the keys to a car, but rather, a brand-new Bible. He was so outraged that he turned and walked away, leaving his father holding the Bible. In fact, he was so bitter, he cut off all contact with his father and never spoke to him again. When his father died, he went to his house to prepare for the funeral and to help get his father's affairs in order. There, sitting on a shelf, he noticed the Bible his father had given him for his graduation years before. He blew off the dust and, with tears in his eyes, opened it for the first time. Much to his astonishment, he found an envelope tucked inside the Bible with his name on it. Inside was a cashier's check, made out to him, for the exact price of the car he had picked out. The check was dated the day of his graduation. In other words, his father had given him the car he wanted, but he had to open the Bible to find out. He never realized what his father had done for him, because he did not open his Bible.

As sad as that story is, we essentially do the same thing when we never open the Book our Heavenly Father has given to us. Inside is something far more valuable than a cashier's check. In it are the words of life. In it is the truth about how to get to heaven. What could be more valuable than that?

God's second cure for heart trouble is this: you are going to heaven. Jesus said, "In My Father's house are many mansions . . ." (v. 2). This is only true for the person who has put his or her faith in Christ. The unbeliever does not have the promise of heaven. No matter what happens to you on this earth, it pales in comparison to this great hope. As 2 Corinthians 4:17–18 tells us,

> For our present troubles are quite small and won't last very long. Yet they produce for us an immeasurably great glory that will last forever! So we don't look at the troubles we can see right now; rather, we look forward to what we have not yet seen. For the troubles we see will soon be over, but the joys to come will last forever. (NLT)

Deep inside, we all long for this place we have never been. C. S. Lewis called this "the inconsolable longing" and said, "There have been times when I think we do not desire heaven; but more often I find myself wondering whether, in our heart of hearts, we have ever desired anything else. . . ."[4] We have a longing for heaven, whether we know it or not.

Heaven is waiting for the child of God; you have His Word on it. And there is only one thing that God cannot do, and that is lie. Jesus has gone to prepare a place for us (v. 2). That is a key element of our comfort. When you will be having guests stay in your home, you prepare the room for them. You might know they like certain books or treats, so you customize the room. You do this so that when your guests arrive, they will feel at home. In the same way, God has prepared a place for you.

I heard about an 85-year-old couple who had been married for almost sixty years and had been killed in a car accident. They had been in good health over the last ten years of their lives, mainly as a result of her interest in health food and exercise. When they reached the Pearly Gates, St. Peter took them to their mansion, which was decked out with a beautiful kitchen and a master bath suite, complete with a sauna and Jacuzzi. As they oohed and aahed over their new residence, the man asked Peter how much all this would cost.

> The Lord Jesus will not
> merely send for us, but will come
> in person to escort us to the Father's house.

"It's free," Peter replied. "This is heaven."

Next, they went outside to survey the championship golf course behind their new home. They would have golfing privileges every day, and each week, the course would change to a new one that represented one of the great golf courses on Earth.

The man asked, "What are the green fees?"

"This is heaven," said Peter. "You play for free!"

Next, they went to the clubhouse and saw the lavish buffet lunch with the cuisines of the world laid out.

"How much to eat?" asked the man.

"Don't you understand yet? This is heaven," Peter replied, with some exasperation. "It's free!"

"Well, where are the low-fat and low-cholesterol tables?" the man asked.

"That's the best part," Peter replied. "You can eat as much as you like of whatever you like, and you never get fat, and you never get sick. This is heaven!"

With that, the man threw down his hat, stomped on it, and screamed wildly. His wife and Peter both tried to calm him down, asking what was wrong.

The man looked at his wife and said, "This is all *your* fault! If it weren't for your blasted bran muffins, I could have been here ten years ago!"

I think quite honestly that this description of heavenly mansions we so often hear is probably not literal in the sense of a Beverly Hills-type mansion. Rather, I think it is speaking of our new bodies that God will give to us when we get to heaven. The Bible says in 2 Corinthians 5:1–2, "For we know that when this earthly tent we live in is taken down—when we die and leave these bodies—we will have a home in heaven, an eternal body made for us by God himself and not by human hands. We grow weary in our present bodies, and we long for the day when we will put on our heavenly bodies like new clothing" (NLT).

Our hearts should not be troubled because, first, His Word is true, second, because we are going to heaven, and third, because Jesus will come again: " 'And if I go and prepare a place for you, I will come again and receive you to Myself; that where I am, there you may be also' " (v. 3). In our fallen world, we find relief for our troubled hearts from the fact that Jesus is coming back to receive us unto himself.

When General Douglas MacArthur left the Philippines in the early months of World War II, he fled Corregidor in apparent defeat. Upon reaching Australia, he sent back the now-famous declaration, "I shall return!" And he kept his promise. Three years later, he stood on Philippine soil and made his second historic statement, "I have returned!"

Jesus has told us that He will come again, and someday, in the not-too-distant future, He will set foot back on planet Earth and say, "I have returned." And it may be sooner than we think. The Lord Jesus will not merely send for us, but will come in person to escort us to the Father's house.

In 1 Thessalonians 4:16–18 we read,

> For the Lord Himself will descend from heaven
> with a shout, with the voice of an archangel, and with
> the trumpet of God. And the dead in Christ will rise
> first. Then we who are alive and remain shall be caught
> up together with them in the clouds to meet the Lord
> in the air. And thus we shall always be with the Lord.
> Therefore comfort one another with these words.

Also, notice that Jesus does not say that He will take us
to himself, but He will "receive us" (v. 3). It is not something
that He will do against our will. He will return for those who
are watching and waiting. Not just the place, heaven, but the
person, Jesus, will be ours!

These three reasons, or three cures for heart trouble
that Jesus offered, can comfort and strengthen us:

1. His Word is true.

2. We are going to heaven.

3. He is coming back for us.

These are promises made only to the child of God
who has received Christ.

Jesus revealed these truths to His disciples with this somewhat mysterious statement: " 'And where I go you know, and
the way you know' " (v. 4). I think Jesus wanted them to ask
what He meant. But Thomas was the only one who was bold
enough to do so.

Thomas has been given the title, "Doubting Thomas,"
but he was really more of a skeptic. The doubter doubts,
even when the facts are clear, while the skeptic looks carefully,
wanting to see for himself or herself. Thomas wasn't one to
let others do his thinking for him. He was really behaving
more like "Honest Thomas" than "Doubting Thomas"

when he said, "Lord, we do not know where You are going, and how can we know the way?" (v. 5).

It seems to me the disciples would act as though they understood when they did not. Thomas was honest enough to speak out and say, "We don't know where you are going!"

Aren't you glad Thomas said that? Thomas didn't understand and said so, causing Jesus to utter this incredible statement, one of Jesus' most famous and profound statements in all of Scripture. Jesus did not rebuke him, but rather took his question as an opportunity to expand His revelation of himself.

God has the cure for your heart trouble.

Jesus said to him, "I am the way, the truth, and the life. No one comes to the Father except through Me" (v. 6).

This statement is one of the, if not the most, controversial aspects of our faith. By believing this, we are saying that Jesus Christ is the only way to God. This belief is not held by the majority of Americans today. But if you believe the words of Jesus himself and think and act biblically, then you must believe that Jesus Christ and His finished work on the cross—not human works—is the basis on which you will get to heaven. As Titus 3:5 says, "Not by works of righteousness which we have done, but according to His mercy He saved us, through the washing of regeneration and renewing of the Holy Spirit." And Acts 4:12 tells us, "Nor is there salvation in any other, for there is no other name under heaven given among men by which we must be saved." Then in 1 Timothy 2:5 we read, "For there is one God and one Mediator between God and men, the Man Christ Jesus."

"But that is being so narrow-minded!" some would say. "As long as people are sincere in their beliefs, they can follow any path they want."

What would you think of an airline pilot who announced just before takeoff, "Ladies and Gentlemen, welcome to flight 293 bound for Honolulu. Our cruising altitude today will be 32,000 feet, and we will be showing an in-flight movie. By the way, I am not sure about this whole fuel thing. I see the gauge is indicating that we don't have enough fuel to reach our destination. But I feel good about this, so don't panic.

It is not just believing that He is the Son of God, but it is also receiving Him into your life.

"Also, I am not really using our navigation devices or any maps today, because I feel that is too narrow and bigoted. We'll just flow with it, because after all, all roads lead to Hawaii.

"One last thing, folks. Don't worry, because I'm very sincere!"

All I would want to know at that point is, "How can I get off this plane? There is a psycho in the cockpit."

Of course, we know it is serious business to pilot a plane. Yet how much more serious is our eternal destiny! God has the cure for your heart trouble. He has the answer to your questions. He has the way for you to get to heaven. So, what do you need to do to know with certainty that you are going there?

First, realize that you are a sinner. Every one of us has broken God's commandments. The Bible says, "For all have sinned and fall short of the glory of God" (Rom 3:23). The word "sin" means "to fall short of a standard" or "to miss the mark."

We have all fallen short of God's standards, because the Bible says, "Be perfect, just as your Father in heaven is perfect" (Matt. 5:48). Who is perfect? None of us.

Also, the word "sin" means "to cross a line." God has set up lines and boundaries, and we all have stepped over those lines willingly. So we all have sinned. This is unquestionable.

It also means no more excuses. Stop blaming your parents, addictive behavior, or someone or something else. Like the man in the Bible, you need to say, "God, be merciful to me! ..."

Second, recognize that Jesus died on the cross for you. When the movie, *The Passion of the Christ*, was released, there was considerable controversy over who was responsible for the death of Jesus. *Time* magazine ran a cover article entitled, "Who Killed Jesus?" The debate was raging. Who is really responsible? Do we put the blame on the Romans? Do we put the blame on the Jewish people? I thought the whole debate was absurd, because I will tell you who killed Jesus: I did. You did. Our sins did. And more to the point, Jesus did not go against His will to the cross. He willingly went, because there was no other way to satisfy the demands of a righteous God that we have offended. Nails did not hold Jesus to the cross of Calvary. Love did—love for you and love for me. Jesus said, "Greater love has no one than this, than to lay down one's life for his friends" (John 15:13). No one forced Him to go to that cross. Christ willingly died for our sins.

Third, repent of your sin. The Bible says that God "commands all people everywhere to repent" (Acts 17:30 NIV). This is missing in many people's so-called conversion. It is not enough to just be sorry for doing something wrong. It is also being sorry enough to change your ways. So if you want to get right with God, you need to let go of your sins. You need to be willing to follow Him and do what He has called you to do.

Fourth, receive Christ into your life. It is not just believing that He is the Son of God, but it is also receiving Him into your life. Jesus said, "Behold, I stand at the door and knock. If anyone hears My voice and opens the door, I will come in to him and dine with him, and he with Me" (Rev. 3:20). And John 1:12 says, "But as many as received Him, to them He gave the right to become children of God, to those who believe in His name." You see, there has to come a moment when you say, "Lord, forgive me of my sin. Come into my life." I can't do that for you. Another Christian can't do that for you. You have to say, "Lord, I need your forgiveness." You must receive Him.

Fifth, do it publicly. Jesus said, "Whoever confesses Me before men, him I will also confess before My Father who is in heaven" (Matt. 10:32). But He also said, "Whoever denies Me before men, him I will also deny before My Father who is in heaven" (Matt. 10:33). The point is, if you want to be a true follower of Jesus, then you need to do it in a public way.

Jesus did not go against His will to the cross.

Sixth, do it now. The Bible says, "Behold, now is the accepted time; behold, now is the day of salvation" (2 Cor. 6:2); and "Seek the Lord while He may be found, call upon Him while He is near" (Isa. 55:6).

The Lord is here right now with us. He is calling some of you to himself. There are some of you who need to get right with God, and I am going to give you an opportunity to do that. There are some of you who have fallen away from the Lord and need to come back to Him. I am going to give you an opportunity to return to Christ. So think about what you are going to do as we have a moment of prayer. And then I will invite you to make your decision.

Everyday **Jesus**

C an you think of someone whom you could never imagine as a Christian, someone so hardened, so resistant, and so far gone that he or she would never follow Jesus Christ? Or perhaps *you* are such a person. Or at least you like to think you are. Maybe you feel as though you wouldn't qualify to follow Jesus.

I was such a person. I was raised in a home plagued by divorce and alcoholism. "The OC" was my stomping ground. I went to school at Newport Harbor High in Newport Beach, California. I got into the party scene, drugs, and drinking, and then suddenly, I came to faith. I can tell you, it was the last thing I ever planned on doing, but thankfully, God had different plans than I did. My conversion was so unexpected that people didn't believe Greg Laurie had become a Christian. Yet when I look back on the decision I made and how some of my friends from those earlier days did not make it, I have no regrets whatsoever—not a single one.

Make no mistake about it: conversion is instantaneous. While the process of growing and maturing spiritually takes a lifetime, the actual work of conversion can take just seconds. This means that as you read this book, you can, quite literally, change within moments. You can be a different person on the inside from who you were before. If you don't believe me, just look around the Christians you know who have had their lives changed.

I want to briefly tell you the story of a man whose life was dramatically changed after one, seemingly short moment of contact with Jesus. He was a man who left his career, wealth, and power simply to become a follower of Jesus. It all happened when he came face-to-face with Jesus Christ, who said two things to him: "Follow Me."

His name was Matthew, and this is his story:

> As Jesus was going down the road, he saw Matthew sitting at his tax-collection booth. "Come, be my disciple," Jesus said to him. So Matthew got up and followed him. That night Matthew invited Jesus and his disciples to be his dinner guests, along with his fellow tax collectors and many other notorious sinners. The Pharisees were indignant. "Why does your teacher eat with such scum?" they asked his disciples. When he heard this, Jesus replied, "Healthy people don't need a doctor— sick people do." (Matt. 9:9–12 NLT)

I would hang out in Newport Beach, just wishing some Christian would talk to me.

I don't know about you, but there are two places I don't like to go: the doctor's office and the dentist's office. (And for me, I only go as a last resort, especially to the dentist.) It is probably because we're afraid of hearing some bad news. So somehow, we mistakenly believe that ignorance is bliss.

A man named Phil went to the doctor, and after a long check-up, his doctor said, "I have some bad news for you. You don't have long to live."

"How long do I have?" asked a distraught Phil.

"Ten," the doctor said sadly.

"Ten *what?* Months? Days??"

The doctor interrupted, "Nine, eight, seven. . . ."

But back to our story. ... Tax collectors were looked upon with great hatred by the Jews. For one thing, they collected taxes from their own fellow Jews for the Romans, who were the occupying power in Israel at the time. To make matters worse, tax collectors would often skim off the top or charge more than what was required, and then personally pocket the profit. It's very possible Matthew did that, but this was not the primary reason he was hated. He was considered a traitor, a turncoat, and a collaborator with Rome. Think of an ambulance-chasing lawyer, sleazy used-car salesman, and telemarketer all rolled into one, and you get the idea. Tax collectors barely ranked above plankton on the food chain. It would be like an American collecting intelligence for Al Qaeda. Matthew had aligned himself with the enemies of his own people. It's as though he had gone out of his way to offend his fellow Jews—and God.

We all know people who will do that. They will go far out of their way to offend, to upset, and to put off. Sometimes it is a cry for attention. And sometimes it is because they are running from what they know is right.

Are you running from God right now—perhaps going out of your way to offend Christians and anyone else? Perhaps you are under conviction, and that is why you do what you do. By conviction, I mean the Holy Spirit is making you more and more aware of your need for Jesus Christ, and you are fighting and resisting all the way. The ones who put up the biggest fight are often much closer to conversion than those who don't fight at all. As it's been said, "When you throw a rock into a pack of dogs, the one that barks the loudest is the one that got hit." Perhaps the reason you are "barking the loudest" or protesting the most is because you are closer to coming to Jesus than you like to let on.

But why had Matthew, also known as Levi, chosen this life-style that would alienate and offend so many? We don't know, but we do know this: he was most likely hated by all—all except Jesus, that is. Matthew's only "friends" would have been other tax collectors.

Maybe you feel as though you are hated. Maybe you are lonely, and you don't even know if you have any real friends to speak of. Maybe you hate the course your life has taken—perhaps you are into drugs, drinking, partying, or something else. You feel as though life has "chewed you up and spit you out." Or, maybe you have thought, "If only I could make the big bucks, then I will be happy."

> ## God is not looking for the religious type. He is looking for the sinner type.

As hip-hop star Eninem once said in an interview, "You gotta be careful what you wish for. I always wished and hoped for this. But it's almost turning into more of a nightmare than a dream. I can't even go in public anymore. I've got the whole world looking at me! To be honest, I really have not had much support from family and friends. Just myself."[1]

And rapper Bow Wow, estimated to be worth more than $50 million, said, "I found out the hard way that you can have everything in the world and still not be satisfied."[2]

Musician Dave Matthews makes $20 million a year from his music and touring, but is he a happy guy? In an interview with *Rolling Stone,* Matthews admitted to being suicidal: "It comes and goes. I don't think that it will ever end. When things inside your head get kind of crazy, and you go, 'OK, let's go through the list of options. … ' " He continued, "I like to drink, a lot—I think it's a healthy thing to do. But I've got a family; and I've got other things that impress me more than another drink. … I may pause, but I don't think I'll ever stop, because forever is a long time."[3]

The lyrics to one of his songs, *Trouble,* perhaps explain why he feels this way:

> Here I stand
> Head bowed for thee
> My empty heart begs you
> Leave me be
> But I confess
> You know too well
> That I have fallen
> Pray your mercy give to me. …[4]

Matthew was a very wealthy and successful man, but he was not happy either. And he had turned his back on the very One who could help him: God. Perhaps something happened that turned him in this direction. Maybe he had been disillusioned by some rabbi or priest. Matthew had been raised to believe, but he turned away, or backslid.

It's amazing how many people will turn away from God at an early age because a minister, priest, or some person who clamed to be a Christian did not behave as one. People will turn away from Jesus Christ today for the same reason (or excuse). In fact, there are two reasons people don't go to church:

1. They don't know a Christian.

2. They do know a Christian.

I personally want to apologize for all the Christians who have not been good representatives of Jesus Christ. But Jesus did not say to Matthew, "Follow My people." Rather, He said, "Follow Me." And He says that to you as well. I have been a follower of Jesus for well over thirty years, and I can tell you He has never been a hypocrite or inconsistent in any way. Sure, fellow Christians have disappointed me at times (and I'm sure

I have disappointed some as well), but Jesus Christ has always been who He promised He was to me, and that is why I am following Him.

The truth is, God loves you, and His plan for you is good.

Matthew would have had a great seat there at his strategically located tax booth. He may have even listened as Jesus taught from a boat. His heart, which undoubtedly had become hardened and bitter by the treatment of others, began to soften. But he couldn't bring himself to get up from that tax booth and go to Jesus. He probably was afraid Jesus would reject him: "Do I actually look so desperate that I would want a tax collector to follow Me?"

I used to be like that. I would hang out in Newport Beach, just wishing some Christian would talk to me, but they never really did. Thankfully, God could see past my hardened façade and called my name—just like He called Matthew's and just like He is calling yours.

You may be thinking, "But I'm just not the religious type." But God is not looking for the religious type. He is looking for the sinner type.

One day, Jesus saw Matthew and said two words that would forever change Matthew's life: "As Jesus passed on from there, He saw a man named Matthew sitting at the tax office. And He said to him, 'Follow Me.' So he arose and followed Him." (Matt. 9:9). The word "saw" in this verse is very suggestive. It means "to gaze intently upon, to stare, to fix one's eyes constantly upon an object." I'm sure that when people walked by Matthew, normally they would either turn away their eyes or look at him with scorn.

This word also means, "to look right through." Have you ever had someone look right through you? Or, let me put it another way: do you have a mother? Jesus intentionally made eye contact with Matthew. And in the eyes of Jesus, Matthew saw many things: holiness and purity, to name a few. But I'm certain he also saw love, compassion, and understanding. With their eyes fixed on each other, Jesus said two words that would reverberate through Matthew's soul, words that he never thought he would hear: "Follow Me" (v. 9). Jesus was choosing, selecting, and calling him out to be His disciple. And Jesus is saying the same thing to you right now.

But what does it mean to "follow Jesus?" There are a lot of us today who claim to be His followers, but are we? As 2 Corinthians 13:5 reminds us, "Examine and test and evaluate your own selves to see whether you are holding to your faith and showing the proper fruits of it. Test and prove yourselves (not Christ). Do you not yourselves realize and know (thoroughly by an ever-increasing experience) that Jesus Christ is in you—unless you are (counterfeits) disapproved on trial and rejected?" (AMPLIFIED).

This phrase, "follow Me," could also be translated, "follow *with* Me," meaning companionship and friendship. Jesus was saying, "Matthew, I want you to be My friend!" Did you know that Jesus is saying the same to you right now? He wants you to bare your heart to Him, to tell Him your secrets, your fears, your hopes, and your dreams. Jesus said, "You are My friends if you do whatever I command you. No longer do I call you servants, for a servant does not know what his master is doing; but I have called you friends, for all things that I heard from My Father I have made known to you" (John 15:14–15).

Many people think God is out to ruin their lives. They believe He is always mad at them. Such was the case with a burglar who broke into a house one night. As he quietly made his way around, a voice suddenly spoke through the darkness: "I see you, and Jesus sees you too."

He stopped, amazed at what he had just heard. He waited for a few moments, and when nothing happened, he continued on.

For a second time the voice said, "I see you, and Jesus sees you too."

Stunned, the burglar turned on his flashlight for a look around the room. To his surprise and relief, he saw a large bird cage in the corner with a parrot inside.

"Did you say that?" he asked the parrot.

"I see you, and Jesus sees you too," the parrot repeated for the third time.

"Why, it's a parrot!" laughed the burglar. But then the burglar saw a large Doberman with its teeth bared, looking at him.

The parrot then said to the Doberman, "Sic 'em, Jesus!"

That's how a lot of people see Jesus: ready to pounce on them and ruin their lives. Nothing could be further from the truth. The fact is, God loves you, and His plan for you is good. God says, "For I know the thoughts that I think toward you,… thoughts of peace and not of evil, to give you a future and a hope" (Jer. 29:11).

Jesus told the story of a prodigal son who demanded his inheritance from his father and then left home and ended up wasting it all on immoral living. When he came to his senses and realized that even his father's servants had it better than he did, he decided to go home. His father, who spotted him coming down the road one day, ran out to meet him and threw his arms around him. He welcomed him home and even threw him a party. This father was overjoyed that his prodigal son had come home.

In the same way, when we have sinned against God, He misses us, just as that father missed his wayward son. God wants to be your friend. The question is, do you want to be

His? There are a lot of people running around today who claim to be friends of Jesus. But if you are a true friend of Jesus, then you will obey Him. Remember, Jesus said, "You are My friends if you do whatever I *command* you" (John 15:14, emphasis mine). It is not for us to pick and choose which parts of the Bible we like and then throw out the rest. What God offers is a package deal.

He is not Sunday Jesus, but everyday Jesus.

When Jesus said to Matthew, "Follow Me," the word "follow" that He used comes from a Greek word meaning "to walk the same road." It is in the imperative, meaning that Jesus' statement was not only an invitation, but also a command. The word is also a verb in the present tense, commanding the beginning of an action and continuing habitually in it. In other words, Jesus was essentially saying, "I command you to follow Me each and every day."

Following Jesus is not something we do only on Sunday. He is not Sunday Jesus, but everyday Jesus. He wants to go with you to church, to school, to work, to the movies, as you surf the Net, and wherever you go.

The Bible tells us that Matthew "Arose and followed Him" (Matt. 9:9). Luke's Gospel adds this detail: "So he [Matthew] left all, rose up, and followed Him" (Luke 5:28).

Matthew, recognizing the immense privilege being offered here, without hesitation stood up and followed Jesus. Do you realize what a privilege it is that Jesus is calling you? As I already mentioned, He called me more than three decades ago as a confused, angry young kid. I wonder where I would be today if I hadn't followed Him.

You may wonder, "If I follow Jesus, will I have to give up anything?" You will give up emptiness, loneliness, guilt, and the fear of death. In its place, Jesus will give you fulfillment, friendship, forgiveness, and the guarantee of heaven when you die. It is God's "trade-in deal," and it is here for you right now.

It would be like hearing a knock at the front door at your home.

"Who is it?" you call out.

"It's Jesus!" a voice replies. "I stand at the door and knock, and if you will hear My voice and open the door, I will come in!"

You quickly open the door, and there He stands: Jesus Christ. You quickly invite Him into your front room.

Nervously you ask, "Could I get you something to eat.Jesus?"

"Of course. Thank you," He answers.

You rush into your kitchen, open the door to the refrigerator, and all that is there is day-old pizza and a few deviled eggs. Somehow these do not seem appropriate. As you are thinking about what to give Jesus to eat, you hear a lot of noise coming from the front room, so you run back in, and there stands Jesus, taking down your pictures from the wall. In the short time you were out of the room, He has already thrown all your furniture onto the front lawn.

Jesus is saying to you right now, "Follow Me."

Now He is proceeding to tear up your carpet, so you cry out, "Jesus, with all due respect, what are You doing?"

"A little spring-cleaning," He calmly responds.

"But Jesus, this is all my stuff here, and frankly, if I would have known you were going to get rid of it, I might not have let You in to begin with!"

He ignores your outburst and gives a loud whistle as He

gestures to the large moving truck backing up to your driveway. Emblazoned on the sides of it are the words, "Father and Son Moving Company."

"Bring it in, boys!" Jesus smiles.

Two very large men lay down the most beautiful carpet you have ever seen. Then they begin to put up color-coordinated, lush wall covering. Then new hand-done works of art are hung in the place of your old ones.

"You have really good taste, Jesus!"

"Yes, I do. Don't forget, I did create the heavens and Earth," He answers.

"Good point there, Lord!" you sheepishly respond.

Then gorgeous, hand-crafted furniture is carefully laid on your new carpet, and suddenly it dawns on you: Jesus only took away the old things to put something better in their place.

When a person really meets Jesus Christ, he or she cannot leave the old life fast enough. Old habits, standards, and practices are no longer appealing and are gladly left behind. But far from being depressed about what he left behind, Matthew's heart overflowed with joy. He lost a career, but gained a destiny. He lost his material possessions, but gained a spiritual fortune. He lost his temporary security, but gained eternal life. He gave up all this world had to offer, but found Jesus.

You may be like Matthew. Maybe you don't have many friends. Maybe you feel alone and empty. Jesus is looking at you right now and saying, "Follow Me."

He offers you the forgiveness of sin, the hope of heaven, and peace instead of turmoil. He offers you friendship and companionship instead of loneliness. He offers you heaven instead of hell. But you must come to Him—not tomorrow, not next week, month, or year, but now. Jesus is saying to you right now, "Follow Me."

You may think, "God could never change someone like me!" But He can—and will—right now. The Bible says, "Therefore, if anyone is in Christ, he is a new creation; the old has gone, the new has come!" (2 Cor. 5:17 NIV). Would you like a fresh start? A new beginning? Would you like never to be alone again?

Or have you, like Matthew, fallen away from the faith? You can come back to Christ today.

People didn't believe that Greg Laurie had become a Christian.

So, what do you need to do to be a true follower of Jesus?

First, realize that you are a sinner. The Bible teaches that "all have sinned and fall short of the glory of God" (Rom. 3:23). That means no more excuses. Stop blaming your parents, addictive behavior, your dog, or your cat. Like the tax collector in Luke's Gospel, you need to say, "God, be merciful to me a sinner!" (Luke 18:13).

Second, recognize that Jesus died on the cross for you. Jesus said, "Greater love has no one than this, than to lay down one's life for his friends" (John 15:13). Jesus willingly died for our sin.

Third, repent of your sin. The Bible says that God "commands all people everywhere to repent" (Acts 17:30 NIV). This is missing in the so-called conversions of many people. Turn from all known sin.

Fourth, receive Christ into your life. It is not just believing He is the Son of God, but it is also receiving Him into your life. Jesus said, "Behold, I stand at the door and knock. If anyone hears My voice and opens the door, I will come in to him and dine with him, and he with Me" (Rev. 3:20).

And the Bible promises, "But as many as received Him, to them He gave the right to become children of God, to those who believe in His name" (John 1:12).

Fifth, do it now. The Bible says, "Behold, now is the accepted time; behold, now is the day of salvation" (2 Cor. 6:2). Matthew made a public stand for Jesus Christ. He got right up from that tax booth and followed Jesus.

It would seem to me that Matthew was more of a backslider than an unbeliever. He was raised in the way of the Lord. He knew the Bible, but rebelled. But when Jesus spoke to Him, He followed.

Have you fallen away from the Lord? Are you living in such a way that if Christ were to return, you wouldn't be ready? God says, "Return, you backsliding children, and I will heal your backslidings" (Jer. 3:22).

Famous **Last Words**

For every person, there will come a last meal, a last breath, and of course, a last statement. And in many ways, what we say in the end is a real insight into what we were in life, what we stood for, and indeed what we lived for. Generally, we die as we have lived.

I read about a man who had been very successful in the restaurant business and had established many restaurants around the United States. When his life was almost over, as he was on his deathbed with his family gathered nearby, he gave his last whisper: "Slice the ham thin!"

Generally, we die as we have lived.

On November 30, 1900, the last words of the famous writer, Oscar Wilde, were, "Either that wallpaper goes, or I do."

Sometimes, people know they are giving their last words. Before he was to be hanged for spying on the British, the last words of American patriot, Nathan Hale, were: "I only regret that I have but one life to lose for my country."

And at other times, people don't know when they will be giving their last words, such as John F. Kennedy, who said, "That's obvious!" This statement was made in response to Nellie Connally, the wife of Texas Governor John Connally. She had remarked to the President as they traveled by motorcade through Dallas, cheered by adoring throngs, "Mr. President, you certainly can't say that Dallas doesn't love you." Seconds later, his life was cut short by an assassin's bullets.

Then there were the last words of William "Buckey" O'Neil, an Arizona lawyer, miner, cowboy, gambler, newspaperman, sheriff, and congressman. He was also one of the most important members of Teddy Roosevelt's Rough Riders during the Spanish-American War. Just prior to the famous charge up Kettle Hill, O'Neil was standing up, smoking a cigarette, and joking with his troops while under withering fire from the ridge. One of his sergeants shouted to him above the noise, "Captain, a bullet is sure to hit you!"

Jesus was held to His cross by love.

O'Neil shouted back his reply: "Sergeant, the Spanish bullet isn't made that will kill me!" No sooner had O'Neil uttered these words when he was hit and killed by a bullet.

Then there were the last words of U.S. tenor, Richard Versalle, who was performing one night at the Metropolitan Opera. Versalle had climbed a ladder for his scene, and after singing the words, "Too bad you can only live so long," immediately suffered a heart attack and died.

And death is no respecter of persons, even for royalty. On her deathbed, Elizabeth I, Queen of England, said, "All my possessions for a moment of time." And Princess Diana, following that horrific car accident in a Paris tunnel, was heard to say, "My God, what happened?"

Some people are in denial about their impending death, like Frank Sinatra, who, as his end was near, told his wife Barbara, "It's none of their d**n business! Dying is a sign of weakness. It's for lesser people. You've got to keep my death a secret. I don't want people gloating. Just bury me quietly. If you don't tell 'em I'm gone, nobody will ever know."

History tells the story of the renowned atheist, Voltaire, who was one of the most aggressive antagonists of Christianity.

He wrote many things to undermine the church, and once said of Jesus Christ, "Curse the wretch. In twenty years, Christianity will be no more. My single hand will destroy the edifice it took twelve apostles to rear." Needless to say, Voltaire was less than successful. And on his deathbed, a nurse who attended him was reported to have said, "For all the wealth in Europe, I would not see another atheist die."

The physician, waiting up with Voltaire at his death, said that he cried out with utter desperation, "I am abandoned by God and man. I will give you half of what I am worth if you will give me six months of life. Then I shall go to hell and you will go with me, oh, Christ, oh, Jesus Christ!"

What a difference faith makes. The last words of Stephen, who was being stoned to death, were, "Lord Jesus, receive my spirit. . . . Lord, do not charge them with this sin" (Acts 7:59–60).

The great evangelist D. L. Moody, on his deathbed, said, "I see Earth receding and heaven is opening. God is calling me."

Now let's consider the most famous and important "last words" ever uttered: the words of Jesus as He hung on the cross. I want to focus on one statement in particular, for in it we see God's most painful moment.

Jesus had been taken to be crucified on the cross, and death by crucifixion was really death by suffocation. It was extremely hard even to breathe, much less speak. Add to this the fact that He had been brutally scourged. The process of scourging was barbaric. The prisoner was tied to a post with his hands over his head, his body taut. The whip had a short, wooden handle with several leather thongs attached, each tipped with sharp pieces of metal or bone. As the whip was brought down on the prisoner, his muscles would be lacerated, veins and arteries would be torn open, and even the kidneys, spleen, or other organs could be exposed and slashed.

Then there was the crucifixion itself, which would cause you to turn away in revulsion at the sight of it. There has never been a movie or painting I've seen that has even come close to depicting what really happened when Jesus died—that is, until Mel Gibson's *The Passion of the Christ.* I don't know that any artist or filmmaker could ever capture all that happened on that day, but this film gives us a glimpse of the incredible suffering Jesus went through for us. Even Gibson has acknowledged that what actually happened to Jesus in His scourging and crucifixion was probably much worse then depicted in his film.

Next to Jesus as He hung on that cross were two criminals who were there for their personal crimes. Jesus, on the other hand, was there for the crimes of all humanity. They were there against their will. Yet Jesus was there because He willingly went. They could not have escaped. But He could have—with just one word to heaven. They were held to their crosses by nails. Jesus was held to His cross by love.

It is fascinating to see how these three men reacted as they looked death squarely in the face. Initially as Jesus was nailed to the cross, these two men momentarily forgot their personal pain and joined the chorus of the onlookers' voices:

> "He saved others; Himself He cannot save. If He is the
> King of Israel, let Him now come down from the cross,
> and we will believe Him. He trusted in God; let Him
> deliver Him now if He will have Him; for He said,
> 'I am the Son of God.' " Even the robbers who were
> crucified with Him reviled Him with the same thing.
> (Matt. 27:42–44)

How this mockery and unbelief must have pained the tender heart of Jesus. Even there at the cross, they persisted, while He was atoning for the very people who were spewing this venom.

In Matthew's account of this event, we read that both thieves joined the crowd in mockery, yet Luke's Gospel tells us that one of them did and was rebuked by the other. Is this a contradiction? No, it is a conversion! Something significant happened to change the heart of one of these thieves, bringing him to his spiritual senses. Initially, he joined the chorus of mockery toward Jesus but then, he watched with amazement as Jesus suffered the same crucifixion as he and the other thief had, yet without any complaint, angry protest, or cursing. Then came those unbelievable, unexpected, incomprehensible words of Christ: "Father, forgive them . . ." (Luke 23:34). These words reverberated through his hardened heart! His rebellion, bitterness, and anger that had no doubt driven him all these years had dissolved. His hardened heart softened.

> He was atoning for the very people
> who were spewing this venom.

While the first word Jesus uttered from the cross was a prayer for His enemies, the second was an answer to prayer, an answer addressed to a single individual. Jesus spoke to Him as though he were the only person in the world. Luke's Gospel tells us the believing thief then said, " 'Lord, remember me when You come into Your kingdom.' And Jesus said to him, 'Assuredly, I say to you, today you will be with Me in Paradise' " (Luke 23:42–43).

In the same way, once you believe in Christ, you can know you are going to heaven. John said, "These things I have written to you who believe in the name of the Son of God, that you may know that you have eternal life . . ." (1 John 5:13).

Can you imagine the joy that must have filled this man's heart? Talk about being in the right place at the right time! You, too, are in the right place at the right time. He will forgive you today of all your sins. He is speaking to you right now as though you were the only person in the world.

There is a lot of debate as to who is responsible for the death of Jesus Christ. Was it the Jewish Sanhedrin and the Pharisees? Was it the high priest, Caiaphas? Was it the Romans? Or Pilate? I will tell you who is responsible for the crucifixion of Jesus Christ on that cross: I was! You were! It was *our sins* that put Him there. Because there was no other way to satisfy the demands of a Holy God, Jesus, who was God, died in our place. The Bible says, "While we were still sinners, Christ died for us" (Romans 5:8). And Paul wrote, "I live by faith in the Son of God, who loved me and gave Himself for me" (Gal. 2:20).

Now the moment comes that Jesus had been dreading. It is here that the tragedy of the Crucifixion reached its horrific climax. In fact, it has been described as "the crucifixion in the Crucifixion":

> Now from the sixth hour until the ninth hour there was darkness over all the land. And about the ninth hour Jesus cried out with a loud voice, saying, "Eli, Eli, lama sabachthani?" that is, "My God, My God, why have You forsaken Me?" Some of those who stood there, when they heard that, said, "This Man is calling for Elijah!" Immediately one of them ran and took a sponge, filled it with sour wine and put it on a reed, and offered it to Him to drink. The rest said, "Let Him alone; let us see if Elijah will come to save Him." And Jesus cried out again with a loud voice, and yielded up His spirit. (Matt. 27:45–50)

Without explanation, the sky turned dark. From the sixth hour (12:00 NOON) to 3:00 P.M., an ominous darkness fell across the land. The Greek word for "land" in this passage could be translated "Earth," indicating the entire world.

Some extrabiblical sources suggest that such a universal darkness did occur. A Roman historian mentioned such a darkness. Also, there was a supposed report from Pilate to the emperor, Tiberius, that assumed the emperor's knowledge of a certain widespread darkness, even mentioning that it took place from 12:00 P.M. to 3:00 P.M.

> When Jesus cried out these words,
> they were not the delusions of a man in pain.

The darkness was then pierced by the voice of Jesus: "My God, My God, why have You forsaken Me?" (v. 46). No fiction writer would have his or her hero say words like these. They surprise us, disarm us, and cause us to wonder what He meant. We are looking at something that, in many ways, is impossible for us as humans to fathom. Clearly, we are treading on holy ground when we look into such a subject, yet the impact on our lives is so significant that it certainly bears looking into. If we can gain a better understanding of what Jesus actually went through for us and what horrendous pain He experienced, it only gives us a greater appreciation for Him and all He has done for us.

When Jesus cried out these words, they were not the delusions of a man in pain. His faith was not failing Him. After all, He cried out, "My God, My God. . . . " As Christ hung there, He was bearing the sins of the world. He was dying as a substitute for others. To Him was imputed the guilt of their sins, and He was suffering the punishment for those sins on their behalf. The very essence of the punishment was the outpouring of God's wrath against sinners. In some mysterious way, which we can never fully comprehend, during those awful hours on the cross the Father was pouring out the full measure of His wrath against sin. And the recipient of that wrath was God's own beloved Son! God was punishing Jesus as though He had personally committed every wicked deed of every wicked sinner. And in doing so, He could forgive and treat those redeemed ones as though they had lived Christ's perfect life of righteousness. Scripture clearly teaches that this did happen: "For He made Him who knew no sin *to be* sin for us, that we might become the righteousness of God in Him" (2 Cor. 5:21). We also read in Isaiah 52:4–5:

> Surely He has borne our griefs and carried our sorrows; smitten by God, and afflicted. But He was wounded for our transgressions, He was bruised for our iniquities; the chastisement for our peace was upon Him, and by His stripes we are healed.

Scripture tells us that "It pleased the Lord to bruise Him" (Isa. 53:10), and we also read that "He himself bore our sins in his body on the tree, so that we might die to sins and live for righteousness; by his wounds you have been healed" (1 Pet. 2:24 NIV).

> The very essence of the punishment was the outpouring of God's wrath against sinners.

Sin, sin, sin was everywhere around Him at this dreaded moment. We cannot even begin to fathom what He was going through at this time. All our worst fears about the horrors of hell—and more—were realized by Him as He received the due penalty of others' wrongdoing.

But to be forsaken of God was as much a source of anguish to Jesus than to anyone else, because He was absolutely, 100 percent holy. The physical pains of crucifixion, horrible as they were, were nothing compared to the wrath of the Father being poured out upon Him. This is why, in Gethsemane,

"His sweat became like great drops of blood falling down to the ground" (Luke 22:44). This is why He looked ahead to the cross with such horror, because never, not for one moment during His entire earthly ministry, did He ever step outside of intimate fellowship with His Father.

Why, then, did this have to happen? Because of the unscalable wall between God and man. God, in all His holiness, could not look at sin, because He is "of purer eyes than to behold evil, and cannot look on wickedness" (Hab. 1:13). As a result, man, in all his sinfulness, could not look at God. So the Holy Father had to turn His face and pour His wrath upon His own Son. Understand that for Jesus, this was the greatest sacrifice He could have possibly made. His greatest pain occurred at this moment. To have felt forsaken of God was the necessary consequence of sin. For a man to be forsaken of God is the penalty that naturally and inevitably follows his breaking of his relationship with God. Jesus was forsaken of God so that I don't have to be. Jesus was forsaken of God for a time so that I might enjoy His presence forever. Jesus was forsaken of God so that I might be forgiven. Jesus entered the darkness so that I might walk in the light. His pain, our gain.

After this three-hour ordeal, Jesus gave His fifth statement from the cross and the first words of a personal nature: "I thirst!" (John 19:28). First, He prayed for His enemies, then the thief on the cross, then He remembered His mother and bore the sins of humanity, and then and only then did He speak of His own needs. Imagine, this was the Creator of the universe making this statement—the One who created water! He could have so easily performed a miracle. After all, He brought water out of rocks in the wilderness. His first earthly miracle during His public ministry was to turn water into wine. He simply could have spoken water into existence.

But it's important to note that Jesus never once performed a miracle for His own benefit or comfort. When tempted by Satan to do this, He refused. Scripture tells us that He was hungry, he grew tired, he wept, and He was in all points tempted as we are, yet without sin (Heb. 4:15). Yes, Jesus was one hundred percent God, but He was also a man. He was not a man becoming God (that's impossible), but God who became a man. He was called "a Man of sorrows" (Isa. 53:3), so no matter how great your need or difficulty, you know He understands. You can cast "all your care upon Him, for He cares for you" (1 Pet. 5:7). Is your body racked with pain? So was His. Have you ever been misunderstood, misjudged, or misrepresented? So was He. Have you had your closest friends turn away from you? So did He.

Jesus then uttered His sixth statement from the cross: "It is finished!" (John 19:30). The storm had finally passed, the cup had been drained. The devil had done his worst, and the Lord had bruised him. The darkness had ended.

The phrase, "It is finished," is translated many ways: "It is made an end of"; "It is paid"; "It is performed"; or "It is accomplished."

What was made an end of? Our sins and the guilt that accompanied them.

What was paid? The price of redemption.

What was performed? The righteous requirements of the law.

What was accomplished? The work the Father had given Him to do.

Jesus Christ then rose again from the dead. He is alive and here right now, wanting to come into your life.

We see three things as we look at the cross.

First, we see that it is a description of the depth of man's sin. It's been said that you can tell the depth of a well by how much rope is lowered. So don't blame the people of that day for putting Jesus on that cross. You and I are just as guilty. It wasn't the Roman soldiers who put Him on that cross; it was your sins and my sins that made it necessary for Him to volunteer this torturous and humiliating death.

Second, in the cross we see the overwhelming love of God. If ever you are tempted to doubt God's love for you, just take a long look at the cross that He hung on for you. Romans 5:8 tells us, "But God demonstrates His own love toward us, in that while we were still sinners, Christ died for us."

Jesus was forsaken of God so that I don't have to be.

Third, in the cross is the only way of salvation. Jesus said, "I am the way, the truth, and the life. No one comes to the Father except through Me" (John 14:6). If there had been any other way to save you, He would have found it. If living a good, moral life would save you, then Jesus never would have died. But He *did* die. Because there was—and is—no other way.

The story is told of a man who operated a drawbridge. At a certain time each afternoon, he had to raise the bridge for a ferry boat, and then lower it quickly for a high-speed passenger train that crossed a few minutes later. One day, the man's young son was visiting him at work and decided to go down below to get a better look at the ferry as it passed. Fascinated by the sight, he didn't watch carefully where he was going and fell into the giant gears of the drawbridge. One foot became caught, and the boy was helpless to free himself.

His father's heart sank when he saw what happened. He was now forced to make the most difficult decision of his entire life. If he ran to free his son, the train would plunge into the river before the bridge could be lowered. But if he lowered the bridge to save the hundreds of passengers and crew members on the train, his son would be crushed to death.

When he heard the train's whistle that indicated it would soon reach the river, he knew he had to face the inevitable. His son was the dearest thing on earth to him. These people on the train were complete strangers. Yet he knew what he had to do. With tears flowing down his cheeks, he pushed the master switch forward. That great, massive bridge lowered into place, just as the train began to roar across the river. As he looked up and watched the train rumble by, he saw businessmen casually reading their afternoon papers, finely dressed women sipping coffee in the dining car, and a little boy enjoying a dish of ice cream. No one looked at the control house. And no one looked at the great gear box.

With wrenching agony, he cried out, "I sacrificed my son for you people! Don't you care?"

> ## Jesus entered the darkness so that I might walk in the light.

The train rushed by, but no one heard the father's words.

This is what happened at the cross of Calvary. God sacrificed His Son for you because He loves you, because there was no other way for you to be forgiven of your sin. The Bible says, "For God so loved the world that He gave His only begotten Son, that whoever believes in Him should not perish but have everlasting life" (John 3:16).

So what do you need to do?

First, admit you are a sinner. Romans 3:23 tells us, "For all have sinned and fall short of the glory of God." We have all broken God's commandments and have fallen short of His standards.

Second, realize that Jesus died on that cross for you. Remember, "while we were still sinners, Christ died for us"

(Rom. 5:8). And, "God so loved the world that He gave His only begotten Son . . . " (John 3:16).

Third, repent of your sin. The Bible says that God "now commands all men everywhere to repent" (Acts 17:30).

Fourth, receive Jesus Christ into your life. John 1:12 tells us, "But as many as received Him, to them He gave the right to become children of God, to those who believe in His name." And Jesus said, "Behold, I stand at the door and knock. If anyone hears My voice and opens the door, I will come in to him and dine with him, and he with Me" (Rev. 3:20).

Fifth, do it publicly. Jesus died on the cross for you publicly, and He promises, "Whoever confesses Me before men, him I will also confess before My Father who is in heaven" (Matt. 10:32).

How to **Change Your Life**

Without question, God loves you deeply and wants to reveal the personal, custom-made plan that He has just for you. He wants to flood your life with peace, joy, and purpose, and ultimately He wants to spend all eternity with you in a place that exceeds your wildest dreams—a place called heaven.

God says, "For I know the thoughts that I think toward you, … thoughts of peace and not of evil, to give you a future and a hope" (Jer. 29:11).

> First and foremost, he wants to keep
> you from coming to Jesus Christ.

But just as surely as there is a loving God who cares for you, there is a hateful devil who wants to destroy you. He is like "a roaring lion, seeking whom he may devour" (1 Pet. 5:8). Jesus, in speaking of Satan, said that he comes "to steal, and to kill, and to destroy" (John 10:10). That pretty much sums up Satan's agenda: to steal, kill, and destroy.

On the other hand, Jesus comes "that [we] may have life, and that [we] may have it more abundantly" (John 10:10).

In Scripture we find the story of a man who had been completely taken over by the power of the devil, a tortured, suicidal, miserable, lonely shell of a man in an absolutely hopeless situation—that is, until Jesus came along.

It shows us the "package deal" Satan has in store for every person who is in his grip. First and foremost, he wants to keep you from coming to Jesus Christ. He may entice you with all the glitz and glamour this world has to offer. It may be greed for the acquisition of things. But once he has you where he wants you, he'll chew you up and spit you out.

The world's idea of fulfillment is a complete rip-off.

Judas Iscariot is the classic example. It's hard to believe, but those thirty pieces of silver looked pretty appealing. Yet once the devil had what he wanted, Judas was cast aside like yesterday's garbage.

The stuff this world offers us can look so cool and so appealing. MTV, for example, has mastered the practice of making bad stuff look good. One of their most popular shows has been *The Osbournes.* The head of the clan is the wacky Ozzy Osbourne of Black Sabbath fame. Ozzy is the parent a lot of kids wished they had, because if some kid were to brag, "My Dad started his own business!", the kid with Ozzy for a father could say, "Oh yeah? Well, my Dad bit the head off a dove *and* a bat!"

Ozzy and his wife Sharon have two kids, Kelly and Jack. Ozzy has been a heavy drug user and drinker, but he has told his kids not to follow his example. But Jack got caught up in the whole drug and drinking scene and, at age 17, entered a drub rehab facility to get help. Jack explained, "I got caught up in my new lifestyle and got carried away with drugs and alcohol." But do you think MTV was quick to do a really clever show about Jack in rehab? No, because they don't want you to see the reality of what sin does. That might scare you off, you see.

Madonna is someone who has "been there, done that."

She has said,

> Take it from me. I went down the road of "be all you can be; realize your dreams," and I'm telling you that fame and fortune are not what they're cracked up to be. I feel I've earned the right to speak my mind in that area. People think, "Easy for you to say," but it's not easy, because in a way I have to say that so much of what I did and fretted over was a waste of time, like worrying about whether I'd be popular or not.[1]

The world's idea of fulfillment is a complete rip-off, and the end result is frightening.

The story before us illustrates these points. And in this story, we see three forces at work: Satan, society, and the Savior. We will see what Satan did in his life, what society offered, and then what the Savior did.

Jesus had to reach this man in Satan's grip. He simply would not be stopped, because He had work to do:

> When He had come to the other side, to the country of the Gergesenes, there met Him two demon-possessed men, coming out of the tombs, exceedingly fierce, so that no one could pass that way. And suddenly they cried out, saying, "What have we to do with You, Jesus, You Son of God? Have You come here to torment us before the time?" Now a good way off from them there was a herd of many swine feeding. So the demons begged Him, saying, "If You cast us out, permit us to go away into the herd of swine." And He said to them, "Go." So when they had come out, they went into the herd of swine. And suddenly the whole herd of swine ran violently down the steep place into the sea, and perished in the water. (Matt. 8:28–32)

As our story begins, we find two pathetic, demented men. In Luke's account of this story, he zeroes in on one of these men in particular. He seemed to be the more extreme of the two: "When He stepped out on the land, there met Him a certain man from the city who had demons for a long time. And he wore no clothes, nor did he live in a house but in the tombs (Luke 8:27). In addition to this, he would beat and bruise himself, as well as cut himself with sharp rocks. He was so strong that when he was put into chains, he broke them.

So here was quite a creepy scenario: a frightening, evil man with superhuman strength, who hung out at the graveyard. No doubt the people avoided this place, especially at night. Superstitious people would have said this was a place for ghosts and goblins. He was a dangerous and frightening man, but underneath that dark exterior was a truly tortured soul. And, as I mentioned earlier, he is a picture of Satan's ultimate goal—the finished product.

What steps led to this state we can only imagine. But here we see the "package deal" of sin, Satan, and death, all intertwined together. What a dark and depressing situation. Sin is indeed a living death, and the unbeliever is spiritually "dead in trespasses and sins" (Eph. 2:1). The Bible says, "But she who lives in pleasure is dead while she lives" (1 Tim. 5:6). But this is a story with a happy ending, because Jesus came into this poor, tortured man's life and made him into an altogether different kind of person.

When Jesus showed up at this place, seeking out these men, Satan reacted with force: "They began screaming at him, 'Why are you bothering us, Son of God? You have no right to torture us before God's appointed time!' " (Matt. 8:29 NLT). The power of Satan was so entwined with this man that most would not have been able to see the hurting person deep inside, but only the crazed, suicidal maniac roaming the graveyard. Yet in this cry, Jesus also may have heard that the man wanted His help.

Your friends may have dragged you here, kicking and screaming. You may have told them, "I don't need Jesus." You are always the first one with the argument and the protesting. But there is a proverb that says, "When you throw a rock into a pack of dogs, the one that barks the loudest is the one that got hit." Perhaps that describes you right now. Despite all your arguments, you are here— because deep down inside, you are searching. You are lonely and afraid.

> They played around with sin, and now sin was playing around with them.

This man did the right thing. He realized that he did not have power, so he cried out to Jesus. And that is what each of us needs to do. The only thing stronger than the power of Satan is the power of Jesus.

The demons possessing this man screamed out a bizarre question: "Why are you bothering us, Son of God? You have no right to torture us before God's appointed time!" (v. 29). James tells us, "Even the demons believe—and tremble!" (James 2:19). It may surprise you to know that the demons, and the devil himself, are neither atheists nor agnostics. They believe in the existence of God. They believe in the deity of Jesus Christ. They believe that the Bible is the very Word of God. They believe Jesus is coming back again. In fact, you could say that, in a very limited sense, demons and the devil are quite orthodox in their beliefs. Needless to say, they are not followers of Jesus.

I remember, as a very young Christian, hearing someone say, "Let's pray for Satan's conversion!" Of course, this is not going to happen. So the point is that it is not enough to simply believe that Jesus was God. Satan does. It is not enough to believe that the Bible is the Word of God. You must personally choose to follow Jesus.

In Luke's account of this story, we read that Jesus asked, "What is your name?" (Luke 8:30).

He answered, "Legion," because many demons had entered him. This man was so wrapped up in demon powers that he couldn't even answer for himself. A Roman legion consisted of six thousand soldiers, which means this man was possessed by perhaps hundreds, even thousands, of demons!

Somewhere along the line, these men had opened themselves up to satanic invasion. They played around with sin, and now sin was playing around with them. They had lost everything. They lost their homes, their family, their friends, and even their will. They were completely under the power of the devil. We must remember this when we start playing games with sin. Satan will dangle what he must in front of you to get you to take the bait.

> I was trying to fill a hole in my heart
> that was made to be filled with God.

There are many who open the door to the supernatural through their use of drugs, as there is a definite link between drugs and the occult. The Bible warns of the sin of sorcery, and in fact, the word "sorcery" comes from the Greek word, *pharmakia,* the same word from which our English word pharmacy is derived. The biblical definition of sorcery has to do with the illicit use of drugs. When people begin to use drugs, whether it's marijuana, cocaine, or any other mind-controlling substance, it opens them up to the spiritual realm.

Dabbling in black magic, witchcraft, Ouija boards, or

astrology can also open the door. The Bible tells us that "those who practice such things will not inherit the kingdom of God" (Gal. 5:21).

I did drugs for a couple of years. I tried the party and drinking scene and thought drugs would do it. They only made my problems worse. I was trying to fill a hole in my heart that was made to be filled with God—not drugs or sex or money or power or anything else this world has to offer.

As I pointed out earlier, we see three forces at work in this story: Satan, society, and the Savior. We've already seen what Satan did with these men. So what did society do for them? They chained them up.

We have a wave of violent crime sweeping across our country. Law enforcement is often understaffed and underpaid. Many of our courts and judges give out lenient sentences. Gangs are growing and spreading. And sadly, the family is continuing to fall apart at an unprecedented rate. Meanwhile, back in our schools, "situational ethics" are taught, asserting there is no right and wrong or black and white, just shades of gray. What is a society to do? Like those in Jesus' day, we just lock people up.

I read an article that pointed to the fact that America's prison population grew to 2.1 million in 2002, a 2.6 percent increase over 2001. In the United States, about one out of every 143 residents was in federal, state, or local custody at the end of 2002. Of those who entered secular drug treatment programs, 95 percent were back using again.[2] With all of its wonderful scientific achievements, society still cannot cope with the problems caused by Satan and sin.

No one could help these demon-possessed men. Their situation was absolutely hopeless. But what the chains could not do, Jesus did with one word. This brings us to the third force at work in this story: the Savior.

What did Jesus do for these men? He sought them out in their spooky little graveyard and offered them hope. And apparently, these demons preferred inhabiting something instead of nothing, so Jesus conceded to their request and sent them into a herd of pigs. The pigs all went over the cliff in madness. You might say it was the first recorded mention of "deviled ham."

What this world can't do, Jesus Christ can.

Luke's account of this story tells us what happened to this man who was delivered: "Then they went out to see what had happened, and came to Jesus, and found the man from whom the demons had departed, sitting at the feet of Jesus, clothed and in his right mind. And they were afraid" (Luke 8:35). What a change!

In the same way, when you look at some Christians, they are so different that you never would know where they had originally come from. If you want proof of the existence of God, then just look at the changes He has made in the lives of Christians you know.

I mentioned that 95 percent of those who entered secular drug treatment programs were using again. Of those who went through Christian drug and alcohol treatment programs, 67 percent were living drug-free, seven years after they had left the program.[3]

I recently met a man from the Czech Republic who shared with me how Christ had changed his life. He told me,

> I grew up in the Czech Republic and in a family where my father was an alcoholic. My first drunkenness occurred when I was three years old, when my father left me in a room with glasses of liquor while he was partying with another guy. They took me to a hospital and found that I had been drunk for fifty hours and

had almost died. I grew up in the communist system. It gave me a rough, hard, and angry attitude. Soon I was known as a fistfighter and an angry man. As I got older, I became even more violent. I went into the military. I spent a short time in prison for violence, alcoholism, and drunkenness. …

He then explained that he moved to the United States and moved in with a woman. He went on to say:

I continued my spiral into alcohol and all the rest of it. On one occasion, my life was spinning down into the bottomless pit. I lost fifty pounds and was ready to commit suicide. I was staring at a gun I was pointing in my mouth. I didn't have any resolve to live. My whole life was one big emptiness, only existing, just a waste of time.

Here is this man, hopeless, alcoholic, violent, and suicidal. And what happened? He continued,

At that time, my neighbor in Mission Viejo and her friends invited me to the Harvest Crusade in 1994. After the music and the message, I knew the Lord was knocking, was on my heart, and wanted me to give up being in control of my life. I got up, walked down to the platform, and asked the Lord to take me out of this garbage and mess, and if He did that, I would do anything He asked. God's Spirit surrounded me and began to melt all of the pain and hurts that I had all of those years, and God's Word started to work in a miraculous way in my life.

He started going to church and learning the Word of God, and now he has gone back to his homeland, has started a church, and is preaching the gospel. What this world can't do, Jesus Christ can.

Jesus delivered the suicidal, tormented, demon-possessed man. So how did the people react? Amazingly, they were afraid:

> Then they went out to see what had happened, and
> came to Jesus, and found the man from whom the
> demons had departed, sitting at the feet of Jesus,
> clothed and in his right mind. And they were afraid.
> They also who had seen it told them by what means
> he who had been demon-possessed was healed. (Luke
> 8:35–36)

The demonstration of the power of God had frightened them. They should have been rejoicing and praising God, but they were afraid.

Guilt comes before repentance, because it shows us our desperate need.

You would have thought they would have asked Jesus to stay with them, but they did the very opposite: "Then the whole multitude of the surrounding region of the Gadarenes asked Him to depart from them, for they were seized with great fear … " (v. 37).

The owners of the swine were angry at Jesus. For some people, after all, Jesus is bad for business. Apparently they felt that something might be required of them. In their case, it was an economic loss. So they decided it would be best for Jesus to go away. Hogs were big business on this side of the lake. Clearly, if Jesus stuck around, it would not be good for business. Two thousand hogs is a lot of bacon, and they now were at the bottom of the lake.

But the fact that Jesus was bad for business wasn't the only reason these Gadarenes wanted Jesus to go away. More than that, they wondered, "If He did that for this one man, would He do the same to us?" Then there was their own guilt. The presence of Jesus Christ always will produce that. They could see in His eyes that He knew everything about them. He seemed to read them like an open book. Just as He cast the demons out of the men and into the pigs, so He seemed able to look through them and see their deepest thoughts. They felt themselves withering in His presence. They were afraid of what He might do. He might want to bring about change in their lives, and they didn't want to change.

But it is important to note that before conversion, there must first come the conviction of sin. Guilt comes before repentance, because it shows us our desperate need. But remember that He who causes us to experience that guilt can also remove it.

Yet they told Jesus to go away. Will you do the same? Really, when you get down to it, this sums up the reaction of all humankind to Jesus Christ. It is either "Away with Him!" or be with Him. We each belong to one of these two groups.

You might protest that and say, "I admit that I haven't made a commitment to Christ and said, 'I want to be with Him,' but I have not said, 'Away with Him!' either. I simply haven't decided yet."

But to not be for Him is to be against Him. Either we pray for Him to go away, or we pray to be allowed to be near Him. Which is it for you?

What are some ways people say, "Away with Him"?

Some reject Jesus out of fear. Perhaps it was one time when they were sitting in church and God began to work on their hearts. They realized this was both true and what they needed. There even was a feeling of joy in knowing this. Yet because of their fear of what their friends would think, or fear of mockery, they resisted and shook off the influence.

They vowed not to go back to church. In essence they said, "Away with Jesus!"

Others reject Jesus out of selfishness. God has clearly shown us in His Word what is right and wrong, but they have decided to do what they want to do. They will continue in that sexual relationship with someone they aren't married to. They will continue partying their lives away. They will continue with that drug or alcohol use. Though God has spoken to their hearts through conscience, friends, and of course, His Word, they are in essence saying, "Away with Jesus!"

Even others reject Jesus because of busyness. This is not as blatant as deliberately breaking His commandments. They just busy themselves with work and anything and everything but Jesus. They're not really busy—that's just an excuse.

Which is it for you? Is it "Away with Jesus!" or "Lord, come into my heart"?

He will not force His way into your life.

Do you know what Jesus did when they told Him to go away? He left. "The entire town came out to meet Jesus, but they begged him to go away and leave them alone. Jesus climbed into a boat and went back across the lake to his own town" (Matt. 8:34–9:1 NLT).

Jesus is a gentleman. He will not force His way into your life. He says, "Behold, I stand at the door and knock … " (Rev. 3:20). He does not say, "I will kick the door in!"

There never has been a better time for you to get right with God than now. The Bible says, "Now is the day of salvation" (2 Cor. 6:2), and "Seek the Lord while He may be found, call upon Him while He is near" (Isa. 55:6).

You may never have another opportunity like this one.

How to **Be Happy**

People today are searching for happiness as never before. I recently saw a television special on the subject, which was called *Happiness: What It Is and How to Get It.* The pursuit of happiness is universal, but I think somehow in the United States, we are even more obsessed with it. It is even mentioned in our Declaration of Independence:

> We hold these truths to be self-evident, that all men are created equal, that they are endowed by their Creator with certain unalienable Rights, that among these are Life, Liberty and the pursuit of Happiness.

But have we found this happiness we pursue? Maybe you have always thought that if you were really rich, then life would be good. I read an article about Jim Carrey, one of the highest-paid actors in the world, which stated, "There's a perception in show business that all comedians are really clowns crying on the inside. And Carrey insists it's true. There is something almost disarming about how up-front Carrey is about past bouts with depression, self-loathing, and even his self-medication through marijuana."[1]

Carrey himself elaborated, "You have to go through your periods where you cry and sob and scream. I've gone on little personal vacations where I'll go away all by myself and sit and curse at the TV for the whole weekend."[2]

Maybe that is why philosopher Erick Hoffer wrote, "The search for happiness is one of the chief sources of unhappiness." A woman is never beautiful enough—in her mind at least.

And the same goes for men. Doesn't it drive you nuts to hear a supermodel discuss the so-called flaws in her appearance? Or, she is reed-thin but insists she needs to lose weight still.

People try to create the perfect body through plastic surgery, and there are even television shows dedicated to the subject, like *The Swan* and *Extreme Makeover.* Why not a show called *You Are Really Ugly, But Just Maybe We Can Fix It?* Actually, I have nothing against plastic surgery, but I would offer just two words of caution: Michael Jackson.

> Happiness comes not from seeking it,
> but from seeking Him.

Added to the pursuit of the perfect face and the perfect body is the perfect wardrobe. Clothes are never fashionable enough. And just when you have revamped your wardrobe to be totally on the cutting-edge, a whole new style comes along.

And of course, you can never have a cool enough house or a fast enough car. On MTV for example, the cameras follow today's stars through their *Cribs,* while another show suggests how cool your life can be if you *Pimp [Your] Ride.* Yet why is it that so many of them are unhappy?

Relationships are never romantic enough. A television special profiled Hugh Hefner and his lifestyle characterized by wealth, power, and women. Yet when asked what was missing, he replied, "I want the words of the songs to be true!"

Life is never full enough. Maybe you find yourself always saying, "I'm bored!"—while you're watching TV, playing the latest videogame, instant-messaging your friends, and talking on the phone. You've tried this drug or that experience, and nothing satisfies. It really never ends. The Bible says, "Hell and Destruction are never full; so the eyes of man are never satisfied" (Prov. 27:20).

Solomon, who pretty much tried it all and had it all, said, "Everything is so weary and tiresome! No matter how much we see, we are never satisfied. No matter how much we hear, we are not content" (Eccl. 1:8 NLT).

A *Psychology Today* article entitled "On the Road to Happiness" pointed out, "Compared to 1960, the America of today has doubled spending power.... The accumulation of material goods is at an all-time high, but so is the number of people who feel an emptiness in their lives."[3]

So where do you find personal happiness? Let me first tell you where you *won't* find it. It will not come from this world. The fleeting happiness this world has to offer comes and goes, depending on your circumstances. If things are going reasonably well, we are happy. If they are not, we are unhappy. But you need to know this: "There are two sources of unhappiness in life. One is not getting what you want. The other is getting it."

I want to tell you a little secret about finding personal happiness. Happiness is not really something that should be sought outright. According to the Bible, if we seek to know God and discover His plan for our lives, we, as a result, will find the happiness that has eluded us for so long. Happiness comes not from seeking it, but from seeking Him. The Bible says, "Happy are the people whose God is the Lord!" (Ps. 144:15). As C.S. Lewis observed, "God designed the human machine to run on Himself."[4]

The Bible tells the story of a rich young guy who had everything going his way. He was incredibly wealthy, powerful, and even moral. But something was missing in his life. He had heard about Jesus and thought He might have the answer to what he was looking for:

Someone came to Jesus with this question: "Teacher, what good things must I do to have eternal life?"

"Why ask me about what is good?" Jesus replied. "Only God is good. But to answer your question, you can receive eternal life if you keep the commandments."

"Which ones?" the man asked.

And Jesus replied: " 'Do not murder. Do not commit adultery. Do not steal. Do not testify falsely. Honor your father and mother. Love your neighbor as yourself.' "

"I've obeyed all these commandments," the young man replied. "What else must I do?"

Jesus told him, "If you want to be perfect, go and sell all you have and give the money to the poor, and you will have treasure in heaven. Then come, follow me." But when the young man heard this, he went sadly away because he had many possessions. (Matt. 19:16–22 NLT)

> The commandments were not given to make us righteous, but rather to show us that we really need help.

Now this guy pretty much had everything the world had to offer. But something was missing in his life.

Maybe you've thought, "If I were just rich, I know I would be happy." When John D. Rockefeller was the richest man in the world, someone asked him how much money was enough. He replied, "Just a little bit more."

Perhaps you have thought, "If I were really rich and famous, I would be happy!" Yet a very well-known Hollywood personality recently said of her peers, "Nobody would be a celebrity if they weren't severely damaged. Honestly, I think we're damaged people and so we're looking for the love we never got. Nobody should look up to us or ever do anything we do. We're basically circus freaks. None of us is altruistic or any of that.

We are pretty selfish and fear-driven people who need help."

This rich young ruler had searched, but had not found, fulfillment in things. So Jesus told him to keep the commandments. The brash guy then had the audacity to ask which ones.

Jesus replied, " 'Do not murder. Do not commit adultery. Do not steal. Do not testify falsely. Honor your father and mother. Love your neighbor as yourself' " (v. 18 NLT).

Some people say, "I live by the Ten Commandments. That's all the religion I need!"

Yet my question for them would be, "Do you? Really?"

It is unlikely that you have committed murder. But let me say that even if you have, God would still forgive you. Of the very men who were pounding the spikes through His hands, Jesus said, "Father, forgive them, for they do not know what they do" (Luke 23:34).

There was a man who hated Christians and went out of his way to hunt them down. He was responsible for the first martyr of a Christian, young Stephen. This man's name was Saul of Tarsus, and he was a murderer. Yet Jesus called out to him on the road to Damascus and forgave him. A man who had once been ruled by hate was now ruled by love.

You may say, "That's good for him, but I have never done anything as horrible as killing someone!" But in the Sermon on the Mount, Jesus takes the idea of murder a step further: "You have heard that it was said to the people long ago, 'Do not murder, and anyone who murders will be subject to judgment.' But I tell you that anyone who is angry with his brother will be subject to judgment (Matt. 5:21–22 NIV). Maybe there is someone who makes you just seethe with anger when you see him or her. Perhaps someone has wronged you or slandered you, and you find yourself hating that person. This is clearly forbidden in Scripture. The Bible says, "Anyone who hates [his brother] is really a murderer at heart" (1 John 3:15 NLT).

The word used for "hates" in this verse means "to habitually despise"—not just a transient emotion of the affections, but a deep-rooted loathing. We have all done that at some time.

> He was possessed
> by his possessions.

Jesus also told this young man, "Do not commit adultery" (v. 18). There should be no confusion as to what this means. However, this wasn't the case with a little boy who attended Sunday School one day, where the Ten Commandments had been the topic. The little boy was a bit confused about the meaning of the seventh commandment. After church, he asked his father, "Daddy, what does it mean when it says, 'Thou shalt not commit agriculture'?"

With hardly a beat between the boy's question and his response, the father wisely replied, "Son, that just means that you're not supposed to plow the other man's field." This would include sex before marriage, as well as sex outside of marriage with someone other than your spouse. There are no exceptions to this. If you commit this sin and do not repent of it, then you will face God's judgment. Hebrews 13:4 says, "Give honor to marriage, and remain faithful to one another in marriage. God will surely judge people who are immoral and those who commit adultery" (NLT).

You might ask, "Why is it so wrong to have sex with someone anyway? So what if you're not married to that person? As long as two consenting adults agree, what's the problem? Why has God laid down a law like this? Doesn't He know that young people have raging hormones and that they will do what they will do? Why is God out to spoil all our fun? What's His problem anyway?"

Know this: God laid down this law for your own good. Think about a couple of basic traffic laws, such as lanes that we are required to stay in, and stoplights. They are a real pain sometimes, aren't they? When traffic is backed up for a mile, wouldn't it be easier to go into the oncoming lane and just pass everyone? Sure. But there is one problem: you could have a head-on collision and kill yourself (not to mention other people). Or, if you are in a rush and the light turns red, wouldn't it be easier to just run it? Sure. But you might find a huge semi pulling out in front of you. Those traffic laws are there for your own good.

Some would say, "Just practice 'safe sex' and it's OK." No, it isn't. The answer is not "safe sex" but to *save sex*—for marriage. There, and there alone, it can be blessed by God. Don't forget that He created it in the first place.

Jesus also told the rich young ruler, "Do not steal" (v. 18 NLT). This is such a widespread problem in our culture today. It has become far more commonplace than we may know. The temptation to steal is constant. When you sell that house or car, there is the temptation to inflate the price to make a little more. When you receive too much change at the store, it's tempting to keep it. Stealing can also be taking office supplies home for personal use or taking help from the government that you don't need.

Not only did Jesus tell this young man not to murder, not to commit adultery, and not to steal, but He also told him, "Do not testify falsely. Honor your father and mother" (vv. 18–19 NLT). Who among us has not broken those commandments? But this brash, and I might add, dishonest, young man said, "I've obeyed all these commandments," (v. 20). But Jesus did not tell him to keep the commandments because he could. He told him this because any honest look at them shows that we all fail and fall short. The Bible says, "For whoever shall keep the whole law, and yet stumble in one point, he is guilty of all" (James 2:10).

> There is nothing this world offers
> that can fill a void that was
> created for God himself.

The commandments were not given to make us righteous, but rather to show us that we really need help. They open our eyes and shut our mouths. As Romans 3:19 says, "Now we know that whatever the law says, it says to those who are under the law, so that every mouth may be silenced and the whole world held accountable to God" (NIV).

But instead of admitting this, this young ruler said to Jesus, "I've obeyed all these commandments. What else must I do?"

Jesus could have said, "You might start with not lying!" But Jesus looked at this guy and loved him. It would appear that this guy was somewhat religious and fairly moral. Yet in spite of that, he knew something was desperately missing in his life. This brought him to Jesus.

So Jesus then told him to get rid of his stuff and follow Him. It's interesting to note that Jesus did not say this to anyone else. Yet He said it to this young man, because he was possessed by his possessions. He had another god before Jesus, and it was his money.

To another, Jesus might say, "You're going to have to break it off with this person. He's been dragging you down spiritually."

To someone else He might say, "You're going to have to put Me first, before your career."

Sadly, this young man demonstrated that things were more important to him than Jesus. The Bible tells us that "he went sadly away because he had many possessions" (v. 22).

This is so tragic that a person could be so close and yet stop short of Jesus. Jesus was offering him the answer to all his problems, and he turned it down.

It reminds me of the following letter I received from a man in Australia:

> Tonight, during Greg's final calls to come forward, I was already standing on the floor, tears in my eyes. Like a bolt from the blue (just for me!) Greg began to relate a story he had read in the *Sydney Morning Herald* about young men today so pressured to "succeed," making fortunes and great careers, appearing to all the world to have all the trappings of success, everything that should ensure happiness. … and he spoke of the high rate of suicide in these same young men. This is me.
>
> After Harvest ended in Newcastle tonight, I walked back to my $100,000 European sports car and drove back to my luxury waterfront apartment. I am typing this e-mail overlooking the lake, sitting on my $12,000 leather lounge, in front of my massive widescreen TV, with my new DVD player still sitting in its box, because I've been too busy to unpack it.
>
> In the next room is a fax with the serial numbers of my new, soon-to-land-in-Australia, $60,000 motorcycle.
>
> In the next room again … is a loaded rifle. It has been sitting there for months, calling me to use it whenever my "great" life (the life that all I know revere and look up to) gets too much to handle.
>
> Thank you … at last I can get rid of that thing! Instead, I now have a Bible to turn to when life gets too much, though I suspect it never will again, now that the HUGE weight of expectation and responsibility—that of others, and mostly myself—has been lifted from me.

Tonight Greg helped save me from a spiral that has brought me very close to both kinds of death and no doubt would eventually have led to the inevitable. I have a rough road ahead—my business partner is a very vocal atheist, just for starters! But I have a peace about it, a lightness of being that I hope stays with me forever and that others will see too.

> Apart from God, you will never find the happiness you are searching for.

The Bible tells the story of another man in a similar situation. He, too, was rich and powerful. He had come to Jerusalem searching for God, but had not found Him. But he heard the message of the gospel from a man named Philip. He believed and was baptized that very day, and the Bible says that "he went on his way rejoicing" (Acts 8:39).

So here you have a stark contrast. Both were wealthy, powerful, searching men. Both were presented with the message of the gospel. One responded and went away rejoicing. One rejected it and went away sad.

You have this same message before you right now. You can go away sad: "I just can't say yes to Jesus." Or you can go away mad: "Don't tell *me* I'm a sinner!" Or you can go away glad: "Lord, I ask for your forgiveness."

You see, the reason you have this emptiness inside is because you were made that way. There is nothing this world offers that can fill a void that was created for God himself. The Bible tells us that He has placed "eternity in [our] hearts" (Eccl. 3:11). We are uniquely made in His very image. All the possessions, success, sex, fame, or power will not fill that void. Only God will.

We as Americans are engaged in "the pursuit of happiness." But listen: apart from God, you will never find the happiness you are searching for. That is because we are separated from Him by our sin. We have all broken God's commandments. We all face His judgment.

You might be saying, "It's worth it. I'm going to just party and enjoy life!" It's what Eminem raps in one of his songs:

I want the money, the women, the fortune and the fame.

If it means I'll end up burning in hell, scorching in flames

If it means I'm stealing your checkbook and forging your name

It's lifetime bliss for eternal torture and pain.

No Eminem, it's not even "lifetime bliss," but it will be eternal torture and pain.

But this is why Jesus Christ died, so we can fill that void deep in our lives and know the God who made us. God loved you so much that two thousand years ago, He sent His Son, Jesus Christ, to die on the cross in your place. He took upon himself the penalty that we should have faced.

You have a choice. You can go away sad, mad, or glad.

If you want that void filled, then you need to turn from your sin and ask Jesus Christ to come into your life. If you want the happiness you have been searching for, it is in Jesus Christ. And you can do that right now.

Yes, the rich young ruler was asked to give up some stuff. But if he would have done it, then what Jesus would have given him in its place would have been so much better! And it will be for you too.

Yes, if you follow Jesus, you will give things up: emptiness for fulfillment, misery for joy, aimlessness for purpose, guilt for a clear conscience, and most importantly, hell for heaven!

We are almost done here. You have a choice. You can go away *sad, mad,* or *glad.* It all comes down to what you do with Jesus Christ.

Immortality

Have you ever had one of those seemingly perfect moments in life when everything just came together? It may have been that stunning sunset, that beautiful, star-filled night, or that special moment with someone you love. You thought to yourself, "I always want it to be this way."

But it isn't.

Maybe you thought when you reached certain goals you have set in life, then that would bring complete fulfillment to you.

But they haven't.

Or when that right person came into your life, the man or woman of your dreams, then that would satisfy the sense of longing deep within you.

But it didn't.

> From the day you were born,
> you have been on a quest.

Why is that? From the day you were born, you have been on a quest. You have been searching for that something more, because deep down inside, there is a sense in you that life must have some kind of meaning and purpose beyond mere existence. Maybe you've even wondered if you're the only person who feels this way.

You aren't.

Deep down inside, we are all searching. Even Madonna.

She once told an interviewer,

I think a few years ago, I wasn't sure what I was on this earth for. I think I was mostly concerned with getting things for myself: more clothes, more money, more popularity, and more boyfriends. I wasn't really thinking; I was just doing. Then I woke up and said, "What am I on this earth for?"[1]

We all want our lives to count for something bigger and greater than ourselves.

Maybe you are wondering, "What am I on this earth for?"

When you are young, you think, "If only I were older, say, 18! The big kids have all the fun!"

When you're 18 you say, "Twenty-one! That's the age I need to be!"

Then when you're 21, you think to yourself, "No one takes me seriously yet. I can't wait until I'm in my 30s."

Then you hit 30. You say, "When I'm in my 40s, then I will have arrived! Those are the earning years!"

Then the 40s come, and you find yourself wistfully wishing you were young again: "I wish I were in my teen years again. Man, we had some fun times back then!"

Then the 50s and 60s arrive. And before you know it, you have more of your life behind you than ahead of you.

It's even funny how we describe the aging process. The terms change with the passing of time. When you are really young, you are "four-and-a-half." (You are never "36-and-a-half.") You want everyone to know you're "four-and-a-half, going on five!"

When you hit those teen years, you're "going to be 16." Of course, you might be 12 at the time, but you're "going to be 16."

Then adulthood finally arrives. You "become 21."
Even the words sound like a ceremony: I've "become 21!"

But suddenly things start going downhill. Yes, you've "become 21," but then you "turn 30." What's going on here?

You "*become* 21," you "*turn* 30," you're "*pushing* 40," you "*reach* 50," and your dreams are gone. Then you "*make it* to 60."

So you "*become* 21," you "*turn* 30," you're "*pushing* 40," you "*reach* 50," and you "*make it* to 60." Then you build up so much speed that you "*hit* 70!"

After that, it's a day-by-day thing. You *hit* Wednesday. And when you get into your 80s, you *hit* lunch. And it doesn't end there.

Into the 90s, you actually start going backward. You're "*just* 92 *years young*."

Then a strange thing happens. If you make it to 100 or more, you become a child again. You're "One hundred-and-a-half!"

Yes, life passes by much too quickly. And sooner or later, every thinking person gets around to asking the questions, "What is the meaning of life?"; "Why am I here on this earth?"; "Why do I exist?"; and "What should be my purpose in life?"

> ## As humans, we were uniquely created in the very image of God himself.

We all have built into us as humans the desire to achieve something, to make a mark, to distinguish ourselves. We all want our lives to count for something bigger and greater than ourselves. This desire for greatness is not in itself wrong. In Romans 2:6–8, we are told that God "will judge all people according to what they have done. He will give eternal life to those who persist in doing what is good, seeking after the glory and honor and immortality that God offers. But he will pour out his anger and wrath on those who live for themselves, who refuse to obey the truth and practice evil deeds" (NLT).

Paul is speaking approvingly of those who seek the "glory and honor and immortality that God offers." God essentially wired us this way. It's built into us. The Bible tells us that God "has put eternity in [our] hearts" (Eccl. 3:11). This verse tells us why we find, deep within our souls, a yearning to rise above the commonplace, the ordinary.

Immortality is not something you achieve, it is something you already have.

But why this desire to make our mark? Because, as humans, we were uniquely created in the very image of God himself. We are the highest of all created beings. We don't want to think that our lives don't matter, that existence is somehow meaningless. We want to live life to its fullest. We want immortality, an endless existence, and enduring fame.

For instance, some people find a certain type of immortality through fame. Everyone knows their name, such as Tom Cruise, Madonna, Britney Spears, and Brad Pitt. Still others are famous for just being famous, like Paris Hilton.

Others find a kind of immortality through becoming infamous, people like Charles Manson, Lee Harvey Oswald, Osama bin Laden, and Adolf Hitler.

Others hope they can prolong their lives by way of all the latest potions and lotions. They are looking for that eternal Fountain of Youth.

I read about a well-known movie star who was once dubbed by *People* magazine as "the sexiest man alive." He has just turned 65 and has lived a hard life of drinking, smoking, and partying. Now he is determined to push back the ravages of time by devoting himself to a so-called anti-aging regimen.

He uses a microscope to study his blood every day. He spends tens of thousands of dollars per year on vitamins and raw food and takes sixty pills daily. But he doesn't just stop with pills. He also uses a syringe to inject himself with other vitamins. He says, "I suppose [that] deep down, there's a passion to live forever. Rationally, I know that's impossible. I know that we all die. I accept the dying process. I would just like to be as healthy as I possibly can at each step and phase along the way."

He is typical of my generation. We baby boomers want to be "Forever Young."

My generation has to update a lot of our songs, by the way. Here are some new title suggestions for a few of them:

The Who: "Talkin' 'bout My Medication"

ABBA: "Denture Queen"

Herman's Hermits:
"Mrs. Brown, You've Got a Lovely Walker"

The Beatles:
"I Get By with a Little Help from Depends"

The Bee Gees:
"How Can You Mend a Broken Hip?"

Crystal Gayle:
"Don't It Make My Brown Hair Blue?"

The Eagles: "Heartburn Tonight"

Jerry Lee Lewis: "Whole Lotta Achin' Goin' On"

Lynrd Skynyrd: "Rest Home Alabama"

Nancy Sinatra: "These Boots Give Me Arthritis"

The Troggs: "Bald Thing"

Yes, life is passing on more quickly than we may like. We all want immortality. But let me say something that may surprise you: Immortality is not something you achieve; it is something you already have. You will live forever.

"That is good news!" you may say.

That all depends. Let's say, for example, that I said to you, "I just bought you a plane ticket to go on vacation for five years, all expenses paid!"

The believer does not need to fear death itself.

You would probably say, "That's great!"

But first you should ask, "Where is this plane ticket to?"

"It is to outer Siberia—in the dead of winter."

You probably wouldn't be too eager to take me up on my offer. But if I were to say the plane ticket was to Hawaii or Tahiti, it would be a different matter.

So our question should not be so much, "*How* can I live forever and be immortal?"

Rather, it should be, "*Where* will I live forever, since I am immortal?"

The Bible has a lot to say about this topic. According to Scripture, you never will die—in a spiritual sense, that is. Man has inside of him a soul, and that soul is eternal. But the body in which we live will indeed die. And all the vitamins, lotions, and potions will not postpone the inevitable.

The question is often asked, "What happens when we die?"

If you have put your faith in Jesus Christ, you will go immediately to heaven. The moment you take your last breath on Earth, you will take your first breath in heaven. It's that fast. Paul said that "to be absent from the body [is] to be present with the Lord" (2 Cor. 5:8).

And in 1 Corinthians 15:53–55, he said,

> For this corruptible must put on incorruption, and this
> mortal must put on immortality. So when this corrupt-
> ible has put on incorruption, and this mortal has put on
> immortality, then shall be brought to pass the saying
> that is written: "Death is swallowed up in victory."
> "O Death, where is your sting? O Hades, where is
> your victory?"

That is why the believer does not need to fear death itself.
This doesn't mean that we Christians have a death wish.
As Paul said, "To live is Christ, and to die is gain" (Phil. 1:21).
Nor does it mean that we don't grieve when we lose a loved
one who is a believer (though a person isn't "lost" if you know
where he or she is). But death no longer has to terrify us.

However, it is a different matter altogether for unbelievers.
What happens to them when they die? They, too, are immortal. They, too, live forever. But where? We find the answer
in Revelation:

> And I saw the dead, small and great, standing before
> God, and books were opened. And another book was
> opened, which is the Book of Life. And the dead were
> judged according to their works, by the things which
> were written in the books. The sea gave up the dead
> who were in it, and Death and Hades delivered up the
> dead who were in them. And they were judged, each
> one according to his works. Then Death and Hades
> were cast into the lake of fire. This is the second death.
> And anyone not found written in the Book of Life was
> cast into the lake of fire. (Rev. 20:12–15)

Note that again and again in this passage, the phrase
"the dead" is used. Back in the Garden of Eden, God gave
the word: "Of every tree of the garden you may freely eat;

but of the tree of the knowledge of good and evil you shall not eat, for in the day that you eat of it you shall surely die" (Gen. 2:16–17). There is no getting around it. Death is coming.

I read of a tombstone in England with this inscription:

Pause now stranger, as you pass by.
As you are now, so once was I.
As I am now, so you will be,
So prepare for death, and follow me.

Everyone will stand before God one day.

Someone reading that inscription was overheard to say, "To follow you is not my intent, until I know which way you went!"

Which way are you going in life—and beyond? According to the Bible, there are only two options after death: heaven or hell. Most of us are afraid to die. The Bible speaks of those "who through fear of death were all their lifetime subject to bondage" (Heb. 2:15). It's the fear of the unknown.

Also note that death is no respecter of persons: "And I saw the dead, small and great, standing before God ... " (v. 12). Everyone will stand before God one day. Not only will we die, but we will face a judgment.

The teaching of a final judgment is clearly taught in Scripture. In Acts 17:30–31, we read, "Truly, these times of ignorance God overlooked, but now commands all men everywhere to repent, because He has appointed a day on which He will judge the world in righteousness by the Man whom He has ordained. He has given assurance of this to all by raising Him from the dead."

And 2 Peter 2:9 tells us, "The Lord knows how to rescue godly men from trials and to hold the unrighteous for the day of judgment, while continuing their punishment" (NIV).

Jesus said, "But I say to you that for every idle word men may speak, they will give account of it in the day of judgment" (Matt. 12:36).

The fact there is a future judgment assures us that ultimately, God is fair. This teaching of future judgment should satisfy our inward sense of a need for justice in the world. We have all seen things that seem so unjust: horrible crimes, wicked actions. We say to God, "How can they get away with that?"

But know this: God is in control. And He keeps very accurate records: "But he who does wrong will be repaid for what he has done, and there is no partiality" (Col. 3:25). Listen! Every wrong in the universe ultimately will be paid for. Either it will turn out to have been paid for by Jesus Christ when He died on the cross (if the offender repents of his or her sins and trusts in Him), or it will be paid for at the final judgment (by those who do not put their faith in Jesus for salvation).

God is in control.
And He keeps very accurate records.

Only unbelievers will be at the Great White Throne Judgment: "He who believes in Him is not condemned; but he who does not believe is condemned already, because he has not believed in the name of the only begotten Son of God" (John 3:18). Yet if the unbeliever is already condemned, then what is the purpose of the last judgment? The purpose of this final confrontation between God and humanity is to clearly demonstrate to the unbeliever *why* he or she is already condemned.

The Bible tells us what will happen at this judgment: "And the books were opened, including the Book of Life. And the dead were judged according to the things written in the books, according to what they had done" (Rev. 20:12 NLT).

One of these books surely will be the book of God's law. Anyone who has been exposed to the truth of God's law is held responsible, "that every mouth may be stopped, and all the world may become guilty before God" (Rom. 3:19). For those who may say, "I lived by the Ten Commandments," it will be clearly shown they did not. We all have fallen short of God's standard for us, which is absolute perfection. "For whoever keeps the whole law and yet stumbles at just one point is guilty of breaking all of it" (James 2:10 NLT).

Perhaps another book will be a record of everything we have said or done. The Bible says, "God will judge us for everything we do, including every secret thing, whether good or bad" (Eccl. 12:14 NLT). And Jesus said, "For every idle word men may speak, they will give account of it in the day of judgment" (Matt. 12:36).

Deep down inside, we all have a sense of right and wrong:

Another book might show how man fails to live up to his own standards. Many years ago, my son Jonathan asked me, "What about the person on a desert island who has never heard about Christ? What will happen to someone like that?" The apostle Paul pointed out that deep down inside, we all have a sense of right and wrong:

> Even when Gentiles, who do not have God's written law, instinctively follow what the law says, they show that in their hearts they know right from wrong. They demonstrate that God's law is written within them, for their own consciences either accuse them or tell them they are doing what is right. The day will surely come when God, by Jesus Christ, will judge everyone's secret life. This is my message. (Rom. 2:14–16 NLT)

Some people say, "I have my own religion, my own beliefs. I'll live by those." But the fact of the matter is that we don't even live up to our own standards we have set for ourselves, much less God's standards!

> ## The main issue on that day will be what you did with Jesus.

Still another book might have a record of all the times you've heard the gospel. And know this: knowledge brings responsibility. I watched a TV program celebrating the tenth anniversary of *Inside the Actor's Studio,* hosted by James Lipton. On each program, Lipton would ask his guests, "If heaven exists, what would you like to hear God say when you arrive at the Pearly Gates?" Here were some of the actors' answers:

"Your friends are in the back.
They're expecting you." (Ben Affleck)

"Come in, have a drink, sit down,
smoke a cigarette." (Ellen Barkin)

"Welcome." (Carol Burnett)

"You see, I do exist!" (Kevin Kline)

"Nice to meet you." (James Caan)

"Everybody you love and all your friends are here!
We already got you a table." (Kevin Costner)

"You're much better-looking in person."
(Harrison Ford)

"Come on in! It's not as boring as you
might have thought." (Richard Dreyfus)

"Fabulous, darling." (Hugh Grant)

"What were you doing down there?"
(Anthony Hopkins)

"I love you." (Val Kilmer)

"You've tortured yourself enough!
Those two hookers and the eight ball
are inside. Come on in!" (Sean Penn)

"Good work, dog!" (Will Smith)

"SHE will say, 'Let's party!' "
(Susan Sarandon)

"If heaven exists, he has a lot of
explaining to do!" (Robert DeNiro)

Hmmm. I think Robert DeNiro will have a lot explaining to do—not God. Many of these answers are quite flippant. I'm sure that will all change when they face God in all His glory. The main issue on that day will be what you did with Jesus. People will offer various excuses as to why they rejected Him. But Jesus put it this way: "Many will say to Me in that day, 'Lord, Lord, have we not prophesied in Your name, cast out demons in Your name, and done many wonders in Your name?' And then I will declare to them, 'I never knew you; depart from Me, you who practice lawlessness!' " (Matt. 7:22–23).

I'm sure that some will say, "But Lord, I went to church on Sunday, received communion, was baptized, gave my confession … " and so on. But you can do all those things and never have known Jesus. Notice Jesus will say, "I never knew you; depart from Me. … "

If you know Him now, He will know you then.
If you walk with Him now, you will walk with Him then.
If you say, "Come in!" now, He will say, "Enter in!" then.

But if you say "no time" or "too busy" or "maybe later" now, He will say, "I never knew you; depart from Me" then.

The Bible says, "And anyone not found written in the Book of Life was cast into the lake of fire. This is the second death" (Rev. 20:15). As it's been said, "Born once, die twice. Born twice, die once." There are no second chances at the second death.

You may ask, "How can a God of love send people to hell? Is this an inconsistency on God's part?"

The fact is, because He is a God of love and justice, He invented hell. But hell was not made for people; it was created for Satan and his fallen angels. God took radical measures to keep us out of hell. Being just and holy, the sin issue had to be settled, because the Bible says, "The soul who sins shall die" (Ez. 18:20).

Born once, die twice. Born twice, die once.

God wants you in heaven. Jesus prayed, "Father, I desire that they also whom You gave Me may be with Me where I am, that they may behold My glory which You have given Me … " (John 17:24). When you're in love with someone, you want them with you. So God poured out His wrath on His own dear Son so that we wouldn't have to face it.

Let's say you were driving on the freeway and were on your way to cross a large bridge spanning a raging river. Suddenly you saw a big sign that read, "Warning! Bridge out! Use alternate exit." But you were determined, so you sped up toward that bridge. As you got closer, you saw more signs: "Do not enter"; "DANGER"; and "Bridge out." Still, you sped on. As you got even closer, you saw police cars with lights flashing and officers waving and yelling for you to turn back. Yet you sped on until you broke through those barriers and went off the top of that bridge into a watery grave. Now, whose fault was it that you died? Was it the construction crew's? The police officers'? No, it was your own fault. You ignored the warnings.

God took radical measures to keep us out of hell.

In the same way, those who end up in hell on that final day will have no one to blame but themselves. God has clearly placed the warning signs. He has told us, "For the wages of sin is death, but the gift of God is eternal life in Christ Jesus our Lord" (Rom. 6:23). As C. S. Lewis said, "No one ever goes to heaven deservingly—and no one ever goes to hell unwillingly."

Every one of us has sinned and will face hell if we do not turn to Jesus Christ. Don't put it off. The road to hell is paved with excuses. Yes, we are all immortal. But the big question is, *where* will we live out that immortality? Heaven? Or hell?

Jesus died on the cross for your sins so you don't have to be afraid to die. He died and rose again. Because Jesus rose, we as Christians will rise too. Jesus said, "I will not leave you orphans; I will come to you. A little while longer and the world will see Me no more, but you will see Me. Because I live, you will live also (John 14:18–19).

God will change your eternal address today if you will turn from your sin.

So what do you need to do to go to heaven?

Admit you are a sinner.

Repent of your sin.

Realize Christ died for your sin.

Receive Him as your Savior.

Do it now.

Epilogue

How to **Know God**

If you want to know God in a personal way, if you don't have the assurance that you will go to heaven when you die, if you are still carrying a load of guilt around, but you want to be forgiven, then here is what you need to do:

1. *Realize that you are a sinner.* No matter how good of a life we try to live, we still fall miserably short of being a good person. That is because we are all sinners. We all fall short of God's desire for us to be holy. The Bible says, "No one is good—not even one" (Romans 3:10 NLT). This is because we cannot become who we are supposed to be without Jesus Christ.

2. *Recognize that Jesus Christ died on the cross for you.* The Bible tells us, "But God showed His great love for us by sending Christ to die for us while were still sinners" (Romans 5:8 NLT). This is the Good News, that God loves us so much that He sent His only Son to die in our place when we least deserved it.

3. *Repent of your sin.* The Bible tells us to "repent and be converted" (Acts 3:19). The word, "repent," means "to change our direction in life." Instead of running away from God, we can run toward Him.

4. *Receive Jesus Christ into your life.* Becoming a Christian is not merely believing some creed or going to church on Sunday. It is having Christ himself take residence in your life and heart. Jesus said,

"Behold, I stand at the door [of your life] and knock. If anyone hears My voice and opens the door, I will come in . . ." (Rev. 3:20).

If you would like to invite Christ into your life, simply pray a prayer like this one, and mean it in your heart:

Dear Lord Jesus, I know I am a sinner. I believe you died for my sins. Right now, I turn from my sins and open the door of my heart and life. I confess you as my personal Lord and Savior. Thank you for saving me. Amen.

The Bible tells us, "If we confess our sins, he is faithful and just to forgive us our sins and cleanse us from all unrighteousness" (1 John 1:9). If you just prayed that prayer and meant it, then Jesus Christ has now taken residence in your heart! Your decision to follow Christ means God has forgiven you and that you will spend eternity in heaven. It means you will be ready to meet Christ when He returns.

To help you grow in your newfound faith, be sure to make the following a part of your life each day: read the Bible regularly, pray, spend time with other Christians by going to church, and tell others about your faith in Christ.

For additional resources to help you learn more about what it means to know God and to be a follower of Jesus Christ, please visit http://www.harvest.org/knowgod/.

Notes

"God's Cure for Heart Trouble"

1. John W. Newcomer; Gregg Selke; Angela K. Melson; Tamara Hershey; Suzanne Craft; Katherine Richards; Amy L. Alderson, "Decreased Memory Performance in Healthy Humans Induced by Stress-Level Cortisol Treatment," *Arch Gen Psychiatry,1999, 56:527-533.*

2. Associated Press, "Poll: Americans Worry about Nuclear Weapons," MSNBC.com, March 30, 2005, http://www.msnbc.msn.com/id/7340591/from/RL.3//.

3. Jeffrey Kluger, "Fear Not!" Time, April 2, 2001.

4. C. S. Lewis, The Problem of Pain (San Francisco: HarperCollins, 2001), 149.

"Everyday Jesus"

1. Brian McCollum, "Eminem on Top: 2002 Brought Giant Success, Steely Focus," Detroit Free Press, December 28, 2002, http://72.14.203.104/search?q=cache:lmjzEbCFZ-0J:www.freep.com/entertainment/newsandreviews/em28_20021228.htm+%EF%82%96%09Brian+McCollum,+%E2%80%9CEminem+on+Top:+2002+Brought+Giant+Success,+Steely+Focus,%E2%80%9D+Detroit+Free+Press,+December+28,+2002&hl=en&gl=us&ct=clnk&cd=1.

2. Teen Vogue, June/July 2004.

3. Rolling Stone, "The Devil and Dave Matthews," January 22, 2004.

4. "Trouble Lyrics," Sing 365.com. http://www.sing365. com/music/lyric.nsf/Trouble-lyrics-Dave-Matthews-Band-and-Dave-Matthews/ED6C178F4706E8E048 256DAB0029FD7D (accessed December 20, 2005).

"How to Change Your Life"

1. Edna Gundersen, "Madonna's Epiphany," *USA Today*, April 17, 2003, updated April 18, 2003, http://www. usatoday.com/life/2003-04-17-madonna-main_x.htm.

2. Curt Anderson, "Growing Prison Population Is Growing Problem for Cash-Strapped States," Associated Press, July 27, 2003.

3. "Addiction vs. Conviction," Christian Counselors Directory, http://christiantherapist.com/ News/111902_01.htm (accessed January 27, 2006).

4. Ibid.

"How to Be Happy"

1. Chris Nashawaty, "Multiple Manic," Entertainment Weekly, June 23, 2000, 28–34.

2. Ibid.

3. John Reich, Ed Diener, "The Road to Happiness; Summary: Five questions for four happiness researchers," *Psychology Today,* July/August 1994, last reviewed August 30, 2004, http://www.psycholo-gytoday.com/articles/pto-19940701-000025.html/.

4. C. S. Lewis, Mere Christianity (New York: HarperCollins, 1980), 50.

"Immortality"

1. "Madonna Reveals Pre-Gig Stress," BBC News, July 3, 2001, http://news.bbc.co.uk/1/hi/entertainment/music/1420364.stm.

About the **Author**

Greg Laurie is the pastor of Harvest Christian Fellowship (one of America's largest churches) in Riverside, California. He is the author of over thirty books, including the Gold Medallion Award winner, *The Upside-Down Church*, as well as *Every Day with Jesus; Are These the Last Days?; Marriage Connections; Losers and Winners, Saints and Sinners;* and *Dealing with Giants.* You can find his study notes in the *New Believer's Bible* and the *Seeker's Bible.* Host of the *Harvest: Greg Laurie* television program and the nationally syndicated radio program, *A New Beginning*, Greg Laurie is also the founder and featured speaker for Harvest Crusades—contemporary, large-scale evangelistic outreaches, which local churches organize nationally and internationally. He and his wife Cathe have two children and live in Southern California.

Other AllenDavid books
published by Kerygma Publishing

The Great Compromise

For Every Season: Daily Devotions

Strengthening Your Marriage

Marriage Connections

Are We Living in the Last Days?

"I'm Going on a Diet Tomorrow"

Strengthening Your Faith

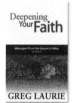

Deepening Your Faith

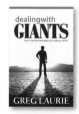

Dealing with Giants

Secrets to Spiritual Success

Visit: www.kerygmapublishing.com
www.allendavidbooks.com
www.harvest.org